The Apostles

by
Evangelist
Bob Sanders

Son Rise Publishing
Kingsport . Tennessee
2000

The Apostles

©

Copyright   2000
Son Rise Publishing
First Printing 2000

*Grateful acknowledgment is given to the following for their
guidance, and help in the development of this book:*
Marlon Thomas
Angie Thomas
Jack O. Cole
Glenda Sanders
Billy Salyers
Angie Jenkins
Mary Ripley

Published by: Son Rise Publishing
3717 Thorngrove Dr.
Kingsport, TN 37660
(423) 288-5773

ISBN: 0-9707309-1-8

Printed in the United States by
Morris Publishing
3212 East Highway 30
Kearney, NE 68847
1-800-650-7888

To

Glenda Smith Sanders

Faithful Friend and Companion of thirty years

Table of Contents

Foreword   *page 7*

Introduction   *page 9*

Chapter One   *page 11*
  The Twelve, Servants of the King
      The Ministry of these Men
      The Makeup of these Men
      The Maturing of these Men

Chapter Two   *page 21*
  Simon Peter, the Transformed Christian
      The Plan for Transformation
      The Process of Transformation
      The Product of Transformation

Chapter Three   *page 36*
  Andrew, the Ordinary Christian
      The Calling of the Ordinary Christian
      The Character of the Ordinary Christian
      The Crop of the Ordinary Christian

Chapter Four   *page 51*
James, the Self-Centered Christian
    The Self-Centered and His Ego
    The Self-Centered and His Education
    The Self-Centered and His Effect

Chapter Five   *page 63*
John, the Loving Christian
    The Communion of Love
    The Communication of Love
    The Commission of Love
    The Consistency of Love
    The Consciousness of Love

Chapter Six   *page 72*
Philip, the Limited Christian
    The Pursuit of God
    The Power of God
    The Purpose of God
    The Person of God

Chapter Seven   *page 83*
Nathanael, the Devoted Christian
    A Place
    A Practice
    A Purity
    A Person

Chapter Eight
Matthew, the Open Christian   *page 91*
    His Mistakes
    His Money
    His Master
    His Message

Chapter Nine   *page 101*

Thomas, the Doubting Christian
    Doubt's Response
    Doubt's Results
    Doubt's Removal

Chapter Ten   *page 118*

James and Judas, the Unnoticed Christians
    Unnoticed But Not Unseen
    Unnoticed But Not Unneeded
    Unnoticed But Not Unrewarded
    Unnoticed But Not Unfaithful

Chapter Eleven   *page 131*

Simon, the Zealous Christian
    The Character of a Zealous Christian
    The Cost of being a Zealous Christian
    The Call to be a Zealous Christian

Chapter Twelve   *page 143*

Judas, the Faulty Christian
    The Covering of the Faulty Christian
    The Crime of a Faulty Christian
    The Cure for a Faulty Christian

Chapter Thirteen   *page 155*

Paul, the Suffering Christian
    The Providence of Suffering
    The Purpose of Suffering
    The Product of Suffering
    The Power in Suffering

Foreword

As Bro. Bob Sanders pastor in his earliest years I watched him as he surrendered to the call to preach, and mature into one of America's greatest evangelists. And as I read his manuscript on "The Apostles", I was convinced that here was a man of sincere convictions and devotedness to the Word of God that would influence many throughout his ministry, and if you've been around him long you'll believe the same.

Many books have been written on the subject of "The Apostles" of our Lord, but in my honest opinion, this is undoubtedly the finest. Dr. Sanders has made an in-depth study of these men, pointing out their mistakes and accomplishments, and in his own unique style has given us an insight into the lives of each of them that excels all other literary works.

I have preached several series of messages on the Apostles as well as other New Testament characters. But after reading Bro. Bob's manuscript I felt I had not scratched the surface.

This book will prove a blessing to every believer whether he be layman, pastor, or evangelist. I am persuaded that your knowledge of the Apostles of our Lord will be much deeper from reading this book.

May God bless each reader as you learn from the mistakes as well as the accomplishments of each of these chosen men known as "The Apostles of our Lord."

Pastor Jack O. Cole DD
Philadelphia Baptist Church
Calhoun, Ga.

Introduction

The Apostles

My purpose is not to give a detailed description of the Apostles lives. There are countless volumes that have very capably accomplished this feat, many of which I have used to research these men's lives. I am deeply indebted to those capable scholars that have gone before. My desire is to take one aspect of each man's life and make personal application to the Christian life. How sad to have a Bible that is historically correct, without error, the spoken Word of God, and have not practical application. I have endeavored to move the truth about these men from our intellect into our daily lives.

While these men were afforded the great privilege of being chosen by Christ to become apostles, they are not without flaws and failures. They have traits that all of us desire to emulate, and they have blemishes we hope do not appear in the lives of our children or ourselves. They were men just like Elijah, *"a man subject to like passions as we are" (James 5:17)*. We too are composed of the same materials.

As we study their lives, may their attributes drive us toward perfection, and may their faults drive us toward purity. May our likeness to them not create pride or despondency but serve as a road map to chart a course to the satisfaction of our Saviour.

Let us not isolate ourselves from these men but stand our lives alongside them. Allow them to become your mentor for greatness and your alarm to corruption. May their lives be used by God to help transform our lives for our good and His glory.

Discover with me:
1. The Twelve, Servants of the King
2. Simon Peter, the Transformed Christian
3. Andrew, the Ordinary Christian
4. James, the Self-Centered Christian
5. John, the Loving Christian
6. Philip, the Limited Christian
7. Nathanael, the Devoted Christian
8. Matthew, the Open Christian
9. Thomas, the Doubting Christian
10. James and Judas, the Unnoticed Christian
11. Simon, the Zealous Christian
12. Judas, the Faulty Christian
13. Paul, the Suffering Christian

May our study prove to be more than mentally stimulating! If this be the case I have failed in my objective. Rather may we move from the darkness of ignorance into the light of divine understanding that fires our soul and causes education to mature into experience.

Evangelist Robert Sanders D.Min.
Kingsport, Tennessee
December, 2000

Chapter One

The Twelve, Servants of the King

Mark 3:14 "And he ordained twelve, that they should be with him, and that he might send them forth to preach,"

The Lord Jesus chose twelve men to continue with Him and to be directed by Him. These men were used to make up a spiritual nation under a new economy established on new principles. While Christ would be the foundation, these men would serve as the early foundational stones of the church. Through the death, burial, and resurrection of the Lord Jesus Christ, these men would do even greater works than the Lord Himself. *"Verily, verily, I say unto you, He that believeth on me, the works that I do shall he do also; and greater works than these shall he do; because I go unto my Father"(John 14:12).*

These men were not gods, rather, they were the servants of the Living God. They were to be His spiritual seed who would bring forth fruit to the glory of God. To say that God used them to make an impact on the known world would be somewhat of an understatement. It was said of one company of the Lord's servants in *Acts 17:6, "these that have turned the world upside down."* I believe that the same could be said of the twelve.

While we do not possess all the gifts of the Apostles for the working of miracles, signs, and wonders, we do have a call to bring forth fruit for the glory of God. *"Let your light so shine before men, that they may see your good works, and glorify your Father which is in heaven" (Matthew 5:16).* Through the working of the indwelling Spirit of Almighty God, we too can impact the world for Christ. The marching orders of the church have not changed just the individual servants called upon to carry them out. May a host of those who are redeemed by the blood of Christ rise up to answer the call.

Much of the Word of God is biographical sketches recorded more for our personal admonishment than historical wool gathering. *"Brethren, be followers together of me, and mark them which walk so as ye have us for an ensample"* (Philippians 3:17)*. "Not because we have not power, but to make ourselves an ensample unto you to follow us"* (II Thessalonians 3:9). *"And turning the cities of Sodom and Gomorrha into ashes condemned them with an overthrow, making them an ensample unto those that after should live ungodly"* (II Peter 2:6). The word "ensample" means an exhibit for imitation or warning, an example or pattern. The record of the twelve is no exception to this truth! A careful study of these men's lives can reap eternal rewards as we seek to duplicate the good and reject the bad.

The Ministry of these Men

What was their purpose? I believe that the shallowness of many Christians is due to the fact that they do not know their purpose! Surely God wanted to do more than just save us from hell and take us to heaven. Many believers remind me of those wind-up toys on wheels that dart across the room until they hit something; then, they change direction and run until their path is blocked; at which time, they change headings again. This continues until they at last run down and are retrieved by their owner. God has a divine plan and purpose for each recipient of His grace. We do not have to run about banging our spiritual heads trying to seek out the will of God.

1. Fellowship with Him

"And he ordained twelve, that they should be with him" (Mark 3:14). Jesus chose twelve men to enjoy personal communion with Him as He performed His earthly ministry. These individuals would listen to His words, observe His walk, and witness His work. John the Beloved put it this way, *"That which was from the beginning, which we have heard, which we have*

seen with our eyes, which we have looked upon, and our hands have handled, of the Word of life" (I John 1:1). For over three years, they would get to know God in the flesh.

God's ultimate purpose for you is to fellowship with Him. In Genesis 1:26, we have this recorded conversation between the Trinity, "Let us make man in our image, after our likeness." Unlike the rest of creation, man was made in the image of God for the purpose of fellowship. Man was given a body, soul, and spirit so that he could interact with his Creator.

While listening to a dear man of God preach on the storm in Acts 27, he read verse 23, "For there stood by me this night the angel of God, whose I am, and whom I serve." He then made the following remark for which I am eternally grateful, "Whose I am comes before Whom I serve." How easy it is to get work before worship, service before supplication, and labor before love! Paul was telling those onboard ship that a relationship of love preceded a request for labor.

Do you have an intimate personal relationship with the Lord Jesus Christ? How rewarding to rise from one's bed in communion with the God of Heaven making melody in one's heart, such as, "He walks with me, and He talks with me, and He tells me I am His own." While we do not always love the one we serve, we always serve the one we love. Much of our labor could be enhanced by simply spending more quality time in personal fellowship with Him.

2. Follow Jesus
To each of these men there was a personal call to follow Him. "And he saith unto them, Follow me, and I will make you fishers of men" (Matthew 4:19). The twelve were not called to follow a movement, rather, they were called to follow a person. This person was not just any person but was God in human flesh, the one that desires intimate communion with them. To know Him is to love Him, and to love Him is to follow Him!

13

The call to follow Christ is still going forth today. *"Then said Jesus unto his disciples, If any man will come after me, let him deny himself, and take up his cross, and follow me" (Matthew 16:24).* I believe there are eighteen references to Jesus saying, *"Follow me."* No matter how long one has been saved or to what heights one has attained, we are to ever be a follower of the Lord Jesus Christ, Paul in writing to the church at Corinth said, "Follow me as I follow Christ" *(see I Corinthians 11:1).* Which one of us has attained in word or work to that of the Apostle Paul? Yet, he remained a faithful follower of Christ. May we sing with the songwriter, "Where He leads me I will follow." There was a story told about a small child that got the words to the song mixed up. He sang, "Where He leads me I will follow, and what He feeds me I will swallow." While the child had the words wrong, the thought was right. May we, without reluctance, follow Him!

The purpose of following Christ is transformation. The words that follow the command to follow are the words of promise, *"I will make you."* The erratic walk and works of many Christians could be cured by simply following Christ. Fellowship and following yields a fashioning. This fashioning is not something we do, rather, it is something that He does in us. When we are faithful to follow Christ, we are transformed into the image of Christ.

3. Further the Work of Jesus

"Verily, verily, I say unto you, He that believeth on me, the works that I do shall he do also; and greater works than these shall he do; because I go unto my Father" (John 14:12). God would commit the work into the hands of mortal men. While on this earth, Jesus said, *"I am the light of the world" (John 8:12),* but before He left, He said to those that had accepted Him, *"Ye are the light of the world" (Matthew 5:14).* His words are to be spoken by us, His work is to be executed through us, and His will is to be accomplished by us.

14

In the New Testament, many were called disciples. A disciple is a learner, one that receives from Christ. The word apostle means a delegate, messenger, he that is sent. The apostle is one that gives forth Christ.

On numerous occasions, we are commanded to, *"Go Ye."* The area we are to work is: all nations, highways and hedges, the vineyard, and the world. The extent of our work is: teach, make disciples, and baptize. In the performance of this work, we have not been left alone. *"For we are labourers together with God" (I Corinthians 3:9).* Every aspect of the Christian life is to be accomplished with Him!

If we are to fulfill our ministry, then, we will find ourselves near Him. This is the only way it can be *"For in him we live, and move, and have our being" (Acts 17:28).*

The Makeup of these Men

Who were these men that were chosen of God to continue the work of God? Were they half god and half man? Did they have super human qualities that made them the chosen of God? These, that were chosen for the ministry, were *"men."* They were just ordinary individuals like you and me. *"Elias was a man subject to like passions as we are, and he prayed earnestly that it might not rain: and it rained not on the earth by the space of three years and six months" (James 5:17).* The twelve were just like Elijah, who was just like you and me, *"a man subject to like passions."* The phrase *"subject to like passions"* means similarly affected. Whether it be Matthew, John, Elijah, Charles Spurgeon, G. Cambell Morgan, or any other servant of the Lord that you hold in high esteem, they were flesh and blood just like you. It does not matter their sex, national origin, or educational status, these, that have left a mark for the honor and glory of God, have the same human defects as you or I.

15

There are three areas that I want us to notice as we contemplate the makeup of these men.

1. They were Born Again
The twelve were made up of those that had responded to the Gospel of the Lord Jesus Christ. *"And when it was day, he called unto him his disciples: and of them he chose twelve, whom also he named apostles" (Luke 6:13).* An individual may be saved and not serve the Lord as they should, but every servant that has impacted this world for the cause of Christ has known what it was to have been born again by the grace of God. There will be individuals that know not the grace of God that advance the popularity of a religious movement or build an earthly ministry for their own glory and financial benefit, but those that exalt Christ as the preeminent Lord and Saviour know Him! *Many will say to me in that day, Lord, Lord, have we not prophesied in thy name? and in thy name have cast out devils? and in thy name done many wonderful works? And then will I profess unto them, I never knew you: depart from me, ye that work iniquity" (Matthew 7:22-23).* Paul encouraged those at Corinth to examine themselves. *"Examine yourselves, whether ye be in the faith; prove your own selves. Know ye not your own selves, how that Jesus Christ is in you, except ye be reprobates" (II Corinthians 13:5)?* Do you know that you have been born again? If you are to ever be an effective servant for God, it is imperative that you have the assurance of your salvation!

2. They were Not Many
I do not know the numerical count of the disciples in *Luke 6:13,* but I know it was greater than twelve because He chose a smaller number out of a larger number. I do know from *Luke 5* that Jesus had become a very popular figure, and the masses were following him about. The crowd was so large that Jesus had to get into a boat and distance Himself from them in order to preach to the multitude of people. It was out of the crowd that He chose twelve.

It pains me to say it, but few will ever commit themselves to surrendering all to serve Christ. When it comes to the work of God, the majority of the work is done by the minority. Most believers are looking for a place to rest rather than a place of service! The fellowship hall is filled to capacity, and laborers for the field are few and far between. Listen to the words of our Lord, *"Pray ye therefore the Lord of the harvest, that he will send forth labourers into his harvest" (Matthew 9:38).* Which group do you belong to?

3. They were Diverse
When we think of the servants of God, most see individuals stamped out like cookies out of a mold. Many have bias opinions that God cannot use anyone that is not just like they are. Others relinquish their opportunity to serve because they do not see themselves like the status quo.

A close inspection of the twelve will reveal that these men were diverse in many aspects of their lives. There was **social diversity** among the twelve. Some came from rural settings and lived on meager fare, while others came from socially prominent families. The twelve revealed **geographical diversity**. Some came from Galilee, while others came from other provinces. There was **educational diversity** to be considered, as well as **occupational diversity**. Jesus enjoyed the variety in those that were chosen to accompany Him. There were fishermen, a publican, a social radical, just to mention a few.

While the quote may have lost its punch, it is still true that the greatest ability is availability. Give yourself unto the Lord to use you in the way that pleases Him. God can and will use you if you will but place yourself upon the altar.

The Maturing of these Men
These men were not ready made vessels when Jesus found them! There would be an educational and developmental process for the twelve. I have learned that it takes God longer to make the

vessel than it takes to perform the ministry for which He created the vessel. Moses' life was two-thirds preparation and one-third operation. Jonah's life was seven-eighth's preparation and one-eighth ministry. Even our Lord prepared thirty years for a three year ministry.

If you are to ever be effectively used for the glory of God, there will have to be a developmental process called maturity take place in your life. For over three years, the twelve were personally tutored by the Lord Jesus Christ. Just as these men grew, we are commanded to grow. *"But grow in grace, and in the knowledge of our Lord and Saviour Jesus Christ. To him be glory both now and for ever. Amen" (II Peter 3:18).*

1. The Cost of Maturity
We are living in a day when everyone wants something for nothing. While that may be what people are looking for, you don't get something for nothing! There is no such thing as a free lunch! There is a price tag attached to maturity, and it must be paid if one is to be an effective servant of the Lord.

Those that followed Christ to maturity left all. *"And he saith unto them, Follow me, and I will make you fishers of men. And they straightway left their nets, and followed him. And going on from thence, he saw other two brethren, James the son of Zebedee, and John his brother, in a ship with Zebedee their father, mending their nets; and he called them. And they immediately left the ship and their father, and followed him" (Matthew 4:19-22). "And after these things he went forth, and saw a publican, named Levi, sitting at the receipt of custom: and he said unto him, Follow me. And he left all, rose up, and followed him" (Luke 5:27-28).* Everything was given up to follow Christ. The twelve released their grip on the world to embrace the Son of God, and each of us must do the same if we are to become His servant.

18

May each of us, with a pure heart, sing with the song writer J.W. Van De Venter, "All to Jesus I surrender, All to Him I freely give; I will ever love and trust Him, In His presence daily live." The price is high, but the rewards are worth it! What is it that you love too much to leave behind and follow Him?

2. The Casting of Maturity
As we have seen, there is great diversity among the servants of God; yet, they became one body under Him. In the maturing process, there were battles with pride. *"But they held their peace: for by the way they had disputed among themselves, who should be the greatest" (Mark 9:34).* When Christ returned unto the Father, a change had taken place among those in the upper room. The phrase *"one accord"* is used repetitively in reference to those that had gathered in the upper room. The phrase means unanimously, with one mind. The followers of Christ had become one. They were cast together in **prayer**. *"These all continued with one accord in prayer and supplication" (Acts 1:14).* They were cast together in a **place.** *"And when the day of Pentecost was fully come, they were all with one accord in one place" (Acts 2:1).* They were cast together in **purpose.** *"And they, continuing daily with one accord in the temple, and breaking bread from house to house, did eat their meat with gladness and singleness of heart, Praising God, and having favour with all the people" (Acts 2:46-47).*

If we are to be effective servants for the Lord Jesus Christ, there can be no division in the body! *"That there should be no schism in the body; but that the members should have the same care one for another" (I Corinthians 12:25). "Let nothing be done through strife or vainglory; but in lowliness of mind let each esteem other better than themselves. Look not every man on his own things, but every man also on the things of others" (Philippians 2:3-4).* The hundred and twenty became one body, with Christ being their head. It is through this body, the church, that God works His will.

3. The Conforming of Maturity

The disciples not only were cast into one, but they were conformed to the image of Christ. In *Acts 4,* Peter and John are brought before the high priest and the religious rulers for preaching Christ crucified, risen, and coming again. As they question and examine these men, there was one conclusion that all came to. *"Now when they saw the boldness of Peter and John, and perceived that they were unlearned and ignorant men, they marvelled; and they took knowledge of them, that they had been with Jesus" (Acts 4:13).* The same crowd that judged Jesus are now looking at His disciples, and they see in them what they saw in Him. That should be the goal of every child of God.

How did this conforming process take place? The answer is simple, they left all and followed Him! You become like those with whom you associate. If we would spend more time with the Living Word and the written word, we too would take on the likeness of God.

Just as the Lord chose twelve men to enjoy intimate fellowship with Him, He is calling us to do the same. As we leave all and follow Him, God begins the maturing process. Soon we are doing the greater works. God has given us biographical sketches of these men's lives to serve as a pattern. As we examine their lives, may we be wooed by the good and reject the bad. May their example help us to become "Servants of the King."

Chapter Two

Simon Peter, the Transformed Christian

Matthew 16:15-18 "He saith unto them, But whom say ye that I am? And Simon Peter answered and said, Thou art the Christ, the Son of the living God. And Jesus answered and said unto him, Blessed art thou, Simon Barjona: for flesh and blood hath not revealed it unto thee, but my Father which is in heaven. And I say also unto thee, That thou art Peter, and upon this rock I will build my church; and the gates of hell shall not prevail against it."

When someone is asked to name the apostles, the name that is most likely to be mentioned first is Simon Peter. There are four lists of disciples in the New Testament, and without exception, Peter is first in each list. Peter was the most prominent disciple because he was a natural born leader. He spoke first, acted first, responded first, and was always standing in the front of whatever was happening. If Peter could have been compared to a part on a car, he would have been the spark plug. Especially in the early part of his life, Peter was impulsive and impetuous. Gaston Foote gave the following description of Peter, "He was a man's man, rugged, rough, and ready for any action necessary to advance the cause to which he had given his allegiance."

Peter was a citizen of Bethsaida which was the fishing capital of Capernaum. He lived there with his wife, mother-in-law, and Andrew his brother. Peter, his brother Andrew, James, and John were professional fishermen and from all indications were partners in the fishing business. Peter, along with several of the other disciples, were followers of John the Baptist.

When searching for the central theme of Simon Peter's life, one is tempted to use words like volatile, unstable, or vacillating. But, this would be only half of the story for there was a transformation that took place in Peter's life. A close study of Simon Peter's life before and after Pentecost would cause one to think you were reading about two different individuals. While there was no physical change in Simon Peter's life, there was a spiritual change! He was not the same person after Pentecost that he was before. Peter was the transformed Christian.

The Plan for Transformation

With the voice of a trumpet, John the Baptist said, *"Behold the Lamb of God" (John 1:36)!* The two disciples with him pursued after the Lord and were invited to see where Jesus was residing. One of those disciples was Andrew, Simon Peter's brother. Andrew sought out his brother and brought him to Christ. When Peter came to Christ, Peter was not aware of the fact that the Lord had great things in mind for him. One thing that God had in mind for Simon Peter was change. There was going to be a transformation in Simon Peter's life. The Lord had no intention of allowing Simon to remain the same individual nor to remain in the same rough state! Peter realized this truth in later years and said in *II Peter 1:4, "Whereby are given unto us exceeding great and precious promises: that by these ye might be partakers of the divine nature, having escaped the corruption that is in the world through lust."* The Lord did not plan on Peter remaining the same and neither does He plan for you to remain in the same state! It is God's will that all His children be transformed.

The Scriptures make it very plain that transformation is the divine plan for everyone that comes to Christ. *"For whom he did foreknow, he also did predestinate to be conformed to the image of his Son, that he might be the firstborn among many brethren" (Romans 8:29). "And be not conformed to this world: but be ye transformed by the renewing of your mind, that ye may prove what is that good, and acceptable, and perfect, will of God" (Romans 12:2).* God's plan is to change your nature into a divine nature by the means of salvation and your character into a Christ-like character by the process of sanctification. Listen to the words of C.H. Waller, "We are not placed in this world into which God has sent us for the sake of anything here. Not for our own enjoyment, not simply for the sake of what we may do while we live. Nor yet only to save our souls from destruction. Nor even to work for God now, that we may rest forever when this life is ended, in eternal contemplation, satisfaction, and praise. We were sent here to form a character, to grow like Him who made us."

The truth of transformation is one that is being neglected in the pulpits of our great nation. The absence of this truth has produced a church filled with anemic weaklings that sport the world's philosophy and dress. This generation's goal is not to be too churchy for the world or too worldly for the church. Thus, we have a mutated Christianity that is void of power but palatable to the unsaved.

1. Change of Name
The plan of transformation is revealed in at least two areas of Simon Peter's life. The first indication of transformation in the life of the son of Jona was in the change of name. *"And when Jesus beheld him, he said, Thou art Simon the son of Jona: thou shalt be called Cephas, which is by interpretation, A stone" (John 1:42).* Today parents are motivated by what they think is cute or innovative when it comes to naming their children. In Bible times, children were given names that gave testimony to their nature, character, or some family trait. This was true in the life of Simon Peter. When the Lord first met Peter, his name was Simon the son of Jona. One writer points out that the name Simon son of Jona has the idea of a fluttering fearful dove. In this name, there appears to be instability and uncertainty. When one examines the early life of Simon, one would have to say that he was living up to his name. It is easy to see the volatility as Simon was confronted with different situations. On two occasions, Jesus stated that there would be a name change for

Simon. Why? There was going to be a transformation in Simon's life. In *John 1:42*, the name is *Cephas*, and in *Matthew 16:18*, the name is *Peter*. In both cases, the names have reference to stone or rock. The transformation in Simon's life would be from instability to that of a solid state.

May I remind you that those who are recipients of eternal life have had their name changed. *"He that hath an ear, let him hear what the Spirit saith unto the churches; To him that overcometh will I give to eat of the hidden manna, and will give him a white stone, and in the stone a new name written, which no man knoweth saving he that receiveth it" (Revelation 2:17). "Him that overcometh will I make a pillar in the temple of my God, and he shall go no more out: and I will write upon him the name of my God, and the name of the city of my God, which is new Jerusalem, which cometh down out of heaven from my God: and I will write upon him my new name" (Revelation 3:12).* Why would God give His children a new name? The answer is a simple one! Because of the transforming work of God in our lives, we have a new nature and a new character which demand a new name. C. Austin Miles was right when he wrote, "There's a new name written down in glory, and it's mine, O yes it's mine." If one has been saved very long, there should already be some changes taking place as evidence of the transforming work of God.

2. Change of Nature
In later years, Peter grasped an understanding of the truth about transformation and wrote, *"Whereby are given unto us exceeding great and precious promises: that by these ye might be partakers of the divine nature, having escaped the corruption that is in the world through lust" (II Peter 1:4).* The phrase *"partakers of the divine nature"* has the idea of being a sharer or companion of godlikeness through the means of growth by germination or expansion. When Peter wrote this verse, I imagine he allowed his mind to drift to the past. He may have thought of all those unstable events, and yet, there had been a

progressive growth in his life. He may not have been all God wanted him to be, but Peter continued to grow more like the Saviour.

Paul emphasized this change in nature in two places when writing to the church at Corinth. *"And as we have borne the image of the earthy, we shall also bear the image of the heavenly" (I Corinthians 15:49).* The word *"bear"* means to wear as clothing or a constant accompaniment. The believer will ultimately wear as a garment and keep constant companionship with a heavenly character. This change is also seen in *II Corinthians 3:18, "But we all, with open face beholding as in a glass the glory of the Lord, are changed into the same image from glory to glory, even as by the Spirit of the Lord."* By using the word *"changed,"* Paul was telling of the transformation or metamorphose that takes place in the life of God's children. When reading what Paul wrote to the Corinthians, one would almost believe that a change was impossible, but this was not the case. It was the plan of God for all His children to bear His image, and they will. *"Therefore if any man be in Christ, he is a new creature: old things are passed away; behold, all things are become new" (II Corinthians 5:17).* Through the divine work of God in the life of the believer, the original nature is going to give way to a new nature!

A careful examination of Simon Peter's early days would cause one to be of the opinion that Peter could never change. He continually moved from one faltering event to another while he topped it all off by denying the Son of God. When others would have given up on Peter, the Saviour did not. There will be transformation in the life of God's children no matter how difficult the task. This truth is revealed in the words of our Lord when He warned Peter of the pitfall Satan had set for Peter. *"And the Lord said, Simon, Simon, behold, Satan hath desired to have you, that he may sift you as wheat: But I have prayed for thee, that thy faith fail not: and when thou art converted, strengthen thy brethren" (Luke 22:31-32).* Jesus did not say to

Peter, "if thou art converted." The words of our Lord were, *"when thou art converted."* Peter's failures were going to be used by God to refine Peter's faith and continually transform the character of His child. Just as the Lord would not give up on Peter, He will not toss you aside. God has given His word when it comes to the truth about transformation. *"Being confident of this very thing, that he which hath begun a good work in you will perform it until the day of Jesus Christ" (Philippians 1:6).* The little children's song says, "He's still working on me," and how true that is! But, we could also say with much assurance, "He is going to work on me." It is this truth that gives us the assurance that we are the children of God. *"God dealeth with you as with sons; for what son is he whom the father chasteneth not? But if ye be without chastisement, whereof all are partakers, then are ye bastards, and not sons" (Hebrews 12:7-8).* The songwriter George Matheson was correct when he wrote, "Oh love that wilt not let me go!"

It is within the program of God that creation, as well as all creatures, go through change. While sin continues to transform the creation and the fallen creatures into a lower state, God is transforming the Christian into the image of His dear Son. He is preparing us for our bright future. May each of us follow the example and admonishment of the Apostle Paul. *"Brethren, I count not myself to have apprehended: but this one thing I do, forgetting those things which are behind, and reaching forth unto those things which are before, I press toward the mark for the prize of the high calling of God in Christ Jesus" (Philippians 3:13-14).*

The Process of Transformation

Transformation was the will of God for Simon Peter, and it is the will of God for all those that have been saved by the grace of God. This transformation process is not an easy one because it demoralizes the flesh and magnifies the Spirit. This process might even be considered part of our spiritual warfare. *"For the flesh lusteth against the Spirit, and the Spirit against the flesh:*

and these are contrary the one to the other: so that ye cannot do the things that ye would" (Galatians 5:17). It is imperative that one remember the nature of this transformation. God was not making a physical change in Simon but rather a spiritual change. Therefore, the instruments that were used in this transformation had to be spiritual. "For though we walk in the flesh, we do not war after the flesh: (For the weapons of our warfare are not carnal, but mighty through God to the pulling down of strong holds;) Casting down imaginations, and every high thing that exalteth itself against the knowledge of God, and bringing into captivity every thought to the obedience of Christ" (II Corinthians 10:3-5).

While there were many things that God used in the life of Simon Peter to bring about Christ-likeness, I want to focus on three of them. These three things were not isolated or just restricted to Simon Peter's process of transformation but are used of God in each of our lives. They are tools to fashion us into the image of God's dear Son.

1. The Indwelling of the Spirit

Jesus took great pains to prepare His disciples for His departure. Christ was returning to the Father and His work was placed into the hands of His disciples. The Lord knew that His work could not be accomplished through the energy of the flesh. In *John 14*, Jesus told the disciples that the third person of the Trinity would be sent from heaven. When the Holy Spirit came, He was not only with them, but He was in them. *"Even the Spirit of truth; whom the world cannot receive, because it seeth him not, neither knoweth him: but ye know him; for he dwelleth with you, and shall be in you" (John 14:17).* The Holy Spirit worked in the life of the believer, conforming them into the image of the Lord Jesus Christ.

How is the Holy Spirit to help conform and bring about this transformation in each of us? Listen to the words of C.H. Waller, "When God pledged His Word to fulfill our destiny, He made it necessary that man should have free access to Himself. We cannot grow like One who will not admit us to fellowship with Himself. From the first, therefore, God pledged Himself to have communion with man. He walked with him in Eden: He bids us walk with Him still." The Holy Spirit is going to continually provide not only access to Christ but encourage communion with Christ. In *John 13-17,* our Lord revealed some of the ways the Holy Spirit provides this access and communion.

The Comforter will provide access to Christ through the ministry of education *(see John 14:26).* This education is in the form of teaching and remembrance. The Holy Spirit will instruct the disciples of Christ in the words of our Lord. He will give us light into the revelation of the Word of God. The truths that we have heard, He will not permit them to lie dormant, but he will remind us of them so that they grow and become functional in our lives. John uses the word *"remembrance,"* which means to remind quietly or suggest to one's own memory. The Comforter will keep the person of Christ ever before us. In *John 16:13,* we are told of the Spirit's guiding ministry. A close study of this verse will reveal that the Holy Spirit will show us the way and announce every detail of things to come. The Spirit of God will not speak of Himself but of Christ. He will provide access and communion with Christ so we may become more like our precious Saviour.

2. The Instruction of the Scriptures
The transformation process is accomplished through the means of natural spiritual growth. One of the means of growth is through the Word of God. *"As newborn babes, desire the sincere milk of the word, that ye may grow thereby" (I Peter 2:2).* The word *"desire"* means to yearn or intensely crave the possession of. As the believer yearns after the Word of God, a supernatural thing takes place. As the child of God begins to possess the Word of God, the Word of God begins to possess them, and spiritual growth takes place. Because the central theme of the Word is Christ, the growth is Christ-like. *"Search*

the scriptures; for in them ye think ye have eternal life: and they are they which testify of me" (John 5:39). Jesus said, "the scriptures testify of me." The Lord was trying to emphasize the fact that the Word of God bore record of or served as a witness of Him.

The Word of God also gives guidance to the child of God as they journey through this world. *"Thy word is a lamp unto my feet, and a light unto my path" (Psalms 119:105).* It is the Word that will lead us in the paths of righteousness for His name sake. It is the Word that will keep our feet from straying or slipping. But, if we do stray into sin, it is the Word that serves as a means to cleanse us and bring restoration in our lives. *"Wherewithal shall a young man cleanse his way? by taking heed thereto according to thy word. With my whole heart have I sought thee: O let me not wander from thy commandments. Thy word have I hid in mine heart, that I might not sin against thee" (Psalms 119:9-11).* God's Word is a tool used by the Holy Spirit to fashion and form the believer into the image of Christ. In the early 1800's, George Muller said "God is the author of the Bible, and only the truth it contains will lead people to true happiness. A Christian should read the precious Book every day with earnest prayer and meditation. But like many believers, I preferred to read the works of uninspired men rather than the oracles of the Living God. Consequently, I remained a spiritual baby both in knowledge and grace." The Word of God generates growth and maturity in the life of God's child.

3. The Illustrations of the Saviour

While the Holy Spirit used the Word of God to transform the life of Simon Peter, He also reminded Peter of the personal illustrations of the Saviour. The Lord Jesus was the perfect illustration of what God wanted out of man and how man was to behave toward his Creator. When the disciples were distraught about the death of the Lord, the Bible says, *"And they remembered his words" (Luke 24:8).* While in this case their remembrance was a source of comfort and reassurance, in other cases it served to instruct and edify them. There were words of compassion as Jesus spoke with those crushed beneath the burden of sorrows. Listen to our Lord as He spoke to a frantic father, *"if thou canst believe" (Mark 9:23)*. Mary and Martha were devastated by the death of their brother and their compassionate friend said, *"I am the resurrection, and the life: he that believeth in me, though he were dead, yet shall he live" (John 11:25)*. The words of Jesus serve as an illustration of how we should speak and control our tongue.

Our Lord illustrated for the disciples how to perform the will of God. *"Jesus saith unto them, My meat is to do the will of him that sent me, and to finish his work" (John 4:34)*. *"For I came down from heaven, not to do mine own will, but the will of him that sent me" (John 6:38)*. It was the will of His Heavenly Father that sent Him to a well in Samaria *(see John 4:4)*. It was the Father's will that caused Jesus to willingly yield to becoming a sacrifice for sin and go to the cross of Calvary *(Matthew 26:39)*. If one desires to pursue the will of God, Christ has given the perfect illustration.

Our Lord also illustrated for us how to walk before God and please Him. Humanity examined the life of our Saviour and said, *"I find no fault in this man" (Luke 23:4)*. Jesus said, *"Which of you convinceth me of sin" (John 8:46)?* There was no one that could charge our Lord with sin. Even the false witnesses could not agree. And then there is the supreme testimony to the pure walk of Christ when the all knowing God said, *"This is my beloved Son, in whom I am well pleased" (Matthew 3:17)*. Our Saviour illustrated for us how to live when it comes to word, will, and walk. May each of us follow His illustrations.

God uses the indwelling Spirit, the instruction of the scriptures, and the illustrations of the Saviour as tools to transform the life of each believer. May each of us yield to the gentle touch of the Master Potter and be conformed unto His image.

The Product of Transformation

When one begins to read the book of *Acts, I Peter,* and *II Peter,* the product of transformation is revealed. Peter was in no way perfect, but oh what a change had taken place. The change has been so radical that one would question if this was even the same man. While the changes are numerous, I want to focus on some outstanding areas of transformation. Peter's transformation could be seen in his relationship to the:

1. Scriptures

When it came to the scriptures, Peter's life was marked by ignorance and intolerance. Just the simple fact that he could never understand the necessity of the cross in the life of Christ revealed his ignorance. He viewed the Messiah as one that would come to set up an earthly kingdom by driving the Roman oppressors from the land. Jesus tried to tell Peter of His impending death on the cross *(see Matthew 16:20-23),* but Peter rejected the truth. This rejection of the truth led to intolerance. In *Matthew 26:31-33,* Jesus said, *"All ye shall be offended because of me this night: for it is written."* What was Peter's response to the Word of God? *"Though all men shall be offended because of thee, yet will I never be offended."* The Word proved to be true and Peter a liar!

There was a big change in Peter's relationship to the Scriptures. Peter had been transformed when it came to the **application of the Scriptures.** As the band of believers waited in the upper room, Peter addressed the subject of Judas. His words were not those of personal opinion but rather the Word of God. *"Men and brethren, this scripture must needs have been fulfilled, which the Holy Ghost by the mouth of David spake before concerning Judas, which was guide to them that took Jesus" (Acts 1:16).* The Word of God was active and alive in the life of Simon Peter. If one will closely read the first three chapters of the book of *Acts,* Peter made reference to the writings of David, Moses, Samuel, and all the Prophets. The Word of God was being applied in Peter's life. This is part of the transforming work that takes place in every believer's life. As we give place to the Word of God in our lives, it changes us, and we give even more room to the Word. This process continues to enlarge itself.

There is also transformation when it comes to **appreciation of the Scriptures.** It is one thing to give place to the Word, and it is another to love the Word. Peter's intolerance was replaced with devotion to the Word of God. In *II Peter 1:4,* Peter makes reference to the Word of God using the terms *"great"* and *"precious."* If Peter was to love the Living Word as he should have, he had to also love the written Word! It is impossible to separate the one from the other. Peter's appreciation for the Word was not only generated out of love for the Saviour but in seeing the treasures it possesses. This is a **powerful treasure**. It is through the Word that we escape the judgment and receive the divine nature *(II Peter 1:4).* It is a **permanent treasure**. Peter said, *"Being born again, not of corruptible seed, but of incorruptible, by the word of God, which liveth and abideth for ever" (I Peter 1:23).* The Word of God will endure forever! How could one not love the Scriptures when its true value is discovered.

Peter also told us of the **acquiring of the Scriptures**. *"For the prophecy came not in old time by the will of man: but holy men of God spake as they were moved by the Holy Ghost" (II Peter 1:21).* Whether Peter knew it or understood it, he then knew that this Book was like none other. These are not just the words of the creature but of the Creator. The third person of the Trinity, the Holy Ghost, moved upon these holy men of old. The Scriptures are nothing less than the inspired, inerrant Word of God! Peter would never be the same when it came to his personal relationship to the Scriptures.

2. Spirit
There had been a mighty transformation within the human spirit of Peter. Peter had changed and would continue to be changed! Salvation will make a radical difference in a person's spirit.

There are two areas of transformation that are very evident in the spirit of Simon Peter.

There was transformation in the area of **fear.** When Jesus started to return to Judaea so that He might raise Lazarus from the dead, the disciples did not want to go. Why? The fear of man. The disciples said, *"Master, the Jews of late sought to stone thee; and goest thou thither again?" (John 11:8)* Fear had so gripped the heart of Thomas, he encouraged the others to accompany the Lord so that they might die with their Master. It was fear that caused Peter to deny the Lord at the High Priest's house. After the Lord had been crucified, it was for fear of the Jews that the disciples huddled in that upper room *(see John 20:19).* Within the spirit of Peter, fear was a driving force. But, a change had taken place. *"Now when they saw the boldness of Peter and John, and perceived that they were unlearned and ignorant men, they marvelled; and they took knowledge of them, that they had been with Jesus" (Acts 4:13).* The word "bold" means outspokenness, frankness, bluntness, or confidence. Peter's feet were standing firm, and his heart was free of fear as he delivered unto them the Word of God. The religious ruler told Peter not to speak at all nor teach in the name of Jesus *(see Acts 4:18).* Peter's answer was, *"But Peter and John answered and said unto them, Whether it be right in the sight of God to hearken unto you more than unto God, judge ye. For we cannot but speak the things which we have seen and heard" (Acts 4:19-20).* The only fear that resided in the heart of Peter was a fear of not pleasing his Lord and Saviour, Jesus Christ.

There was the transformation of **pride.** In the early years, Peter was filled with pride. There was a consistent battle waged among the disciples on who was to be the greatest. When Jesus told of being forsaken by all, Peter said, *"Yet, will I never be offended," "Yet, will I not deny thee" (Matthew 26:33,35).* Peter was filled with self. There was nothing he would not and could not do within himself. Pride had been replaced by humility in the life of Simon Peter. When writing his second epistle, Peter opened by describing himself as a servant. Servant means a slave, therefore in a qualified sense of subjection or subserviency, a bond slave. Peter saw himself as no one worthy of a throne but as one only fit to serve the King of Kings and the Lord of Lords.

3. Speech

In studying the life of Peter, it does not take long to realize that Peter had no control over his tongue. One might say, "If Peter thought it, he said it." It's worse than that, he didn't even think!

There was a transformation in the **subject of his speech.** As I went back and read the different accounts in Peter's life, I noticed a recurring habit. The subject of Peter's speech was mostly himself. Peter was consistently using the personal pronouns I and me. Listen to these repetitive phrases; *"bid me," "I go fishing," "will I never" (Matthew 14:28, John 21:3, & Matthew 26:33).* Yet, when one reads the first four chapters of *Acts* and *I & II Peter,* the subject of Peter's speech was the Saviour. An example of this is *Acts 2:36, "Therefore let all the house of Israel know assuredly, that God hath made that same Jesus, whom ye have crucified, both Lord and Christ."* Christ was now the subject of everything, and Peter was nothing. The subject of our speech should be transformed from self to the Saviour!

There was a transformation in the **suddenness of his speech.** Peter was guilty of engaging his mouth before he engaged his brain. There are two passages that serve as prime examples of this. Along with James and John, Peter accompanied the Lord into the mount. While they were there, Jesus was transfigured before their eyes. Jesus met with Moses and Elijah to speak about His death on the cross. In response to this event Peter blurted out these words, *"Master, it is good for us to be here: and let us make three tabernacles; one for thee, and one for Moses, and one for Elias" (Luke 9:33).* The Word of God had this to say about the suddenness of Peter's speech, *"not knowing* *what he said."* Another example is when the Lord took the place of a servant and began to wash the disciple's feet. What happened when the Lord came to Peter? *"Thou shalt never wash my feet" (John 13:8).* It has been said, "Better to be silent and thought a fool than open one's mouth and prove it." We are admonished in the Word, *"Wherefore, my beloved brethren, let every man be swift to hear, slow to speak" (James 1:19).* Peter was not so quick to speak in the later years. He then allowed the Holy Spirit to tell him when to speak and what to speak. Who is in control of our tongue?

If you are saved, there will be a transformation in your life. There will be a change in your **relationship to the Scripture**, a **reconstruction in your spirit**, and a **restraint on your tongue**. These are but a few of the changes that took place in the life of Simon Peter.

Of all the Apostles, Peter was probably the most familiar. Most relate to Peter's life and have no trouble identifying with him. Yet, most of the identification is with the early years of Peter's life. Why is there not a desire to be like or identify with the transformed Simon Peter rather than the old Simon Peter? J. Golder Burns said of Simon Peter's life, "This is a message to us all. Sainthood is very seldom ready-made. It is the last stage in a long process, the beginnings of which go back into early years, and the succeeding steps of which have been won not without much toil and many prayers and tears." May each of us yield to the tools of the Master Potter as He transforms us into a vessel that will glorify the Saviour and cause our lives to be of the utmost usefulness.

Chapter Three

Andrew, the Ordinary Christian

Matthew 10:1-2 "And when he had called unto him his twelve disciples, he gave them power against unclean spirits, to cast them out, and to heal all manner of sickness and all manner of disease. Now the names of the twelve apostles are these; The first, Simon, who is called Peter, and Andrew his brother; James the son of Zebedee, and John his brother;"
Matthew 25:14-15 "For the kingdom of heaven is as a man travelling into a far country, who called his own servants, and delivered unto them his goods. And unto one he gave five talents, to another two, and to another one; to every man according to his several ability; and straightway took his journey."

Andrew was a native of Galilee, born in Bethsaida. Andrew and Peter, his brother, were partners in the fishing business. It is while conducting the business of fishing that Jesus calls the two brothers to follow Him. Andrew's eagerness toward the things of God can be seen by the fact that he was a disciple of John the Baptist.

As one reads and studies the life of the Apostle Andrew, I find the words of Griffith Thomas a precise portrait of this man, "Andrew is the type of the ordinary Christian. He is not credited with possession of extraordinary gifts." In his book, "The Chosen Twelve," J. Golder Burns deals with Simon Peter and then with Andrew. He opens the chapter on Andrew with these words, "In passing to Andrew, it may not be untrue to say that we descend to a more ordinary level. We can discover nothing brilliant or even showy about Andrew."

I have a feeling that, while most of us do not relish the thought, most of us find ourselves in this category. We are not the despondent, "one talented individual," nor are we the elated, "five talented individual." We are just the ordinary, "two talented Christian."

Most of us will never attain any great notoriety in this world. Our name will not become a household word. We will not be called repetitively to the platform to display or to be recognized for our talents. Those of us that are preachers will not stand and preach to great masses. We will not have to tell folks that our schedule is full for this year and most of next year. Why? We are just the ordinary, "two talented Christian."

While each of us can relate to the hoof and mouth disease that Simon Peter had, we can readily identify with Andrew, the ordinary Christian, also.

The Calling of the Ordinary Christian

In all four lists of the Apostles (*Matthew 10:2-5, Mark 3:16-19, Luke 6:14-16, & Acts 1:13*), Andrew is always listed in the top four. Most writers divide the twelve into three groups of four. While always in the top four, Andrew never makes the top three. The top three had the privilege of seeing Jesus raise Jairus' daughter from the dead. It was Peter, James, and John that went into the mount of transfiguration and saw the glory of God. While all the apostles but Judas accompanied Jesus to the garden to pray, it was the big three that went a little farther. They were permitted to get close enough to hear our Lord's prayer.

Andrew tottered on the edge of being part of that elite crowd, that inner circle that saw, heard, and experienced a little more of the glory. Andrew relates to Benaiah in *I Chronicles 11:25, "Behold, he was honourable among the thirty, but attained not to the first three: and David set him over his guard."*

When one examines the station of an individual in life, it is imperative that one remembers the sovereignty of God. The calling of Andrew to his place of service is left entirely to the Lord! Your abilities and place of service is God's choosing. This truth can be seen and understood in the distribution of the talents in *Matthew 25:15.* When the good man of the house prepared to leave for the far country, the distribution of talents were according to:

1. The Master's Will
The master of the house called in three servants for the purpose of placing his wealth into their hands. He did not divide the wealth and the responsibility of it equally. To one he gave five, to one he gave two, and to another he gave one. Why did he not divide everything equally? The master did not want to and did not have to! His disbursement was in accordance to his will.

When one begins to question their position in life, God's will is not an answer one wants to hear. While we do not like to admit it, sometimes we want to usurp our will over God's will. The nature of the first Adam is "me first," or "I want it my way." The nature of the last Adam is "God first." When the disciples heard Jesus praying to the Heavenly Father, they said, *"Lord, teach us to pray" (Luke 11:1).* Jesus delivered to the disciples what many call the Lord's prayer. One aspect of that prayer was, *"Thy kingdom come. Thy will be done, as in heaven, so in earth" (Luke 11:2).* Jesus taught his disciples to pray that the will of God be done on earth. It must be the desire of each of us that God's will be accomplished in our lives. While we must have the power of the Holy Spirit to accomplish that will, it begins by being yielded to His will.

2. The Master's Wisdom
There is an interesting phrase in *verse 15* that is often overlooked by many, *"to every man according to his several ability."* There are two words that we need to draw our attention

to, *"several"* and *"ability."* The master's wisdom extended to the servant's **person** and the servant's **power**. The word several means one's own, private, or separate. The master had knowledge of each one of his servants personally. We must remember that God sees each of us as individuals. While we are all lumped into the mass of humanity, our God has personal knowledge about each of us. He knows your thoughts, desires, interests, goals, and intents of your heart. He has placed you where you are because He knows you, not because he does not know you. The master had full knowledge of each servant's ability. The word ability means force, strength, or power. God knows exactly what you are capable of doing and what would over tax your power or strength. *"For he knoweth our frame; he remembereth that we are dust" (Psalm 103:14).* When you think God is withholding blessings, it could be that he has chosen to withhold that which would become a burden. What you may think you need for spiritual health may be the very thing that generates havoc and hurt. We must remember that God lives in the eternal with full knowledge, and we live in the temporal with limited knowledge.

3. The Master's Wealth

When it comes to the servants and what each received, we must remember that the wealth was the property of the master. The **servants** were part of the wealth of the master. *"What? know ye not that your body is the temple of the Holy Ghost which is in you, which ye have of God, and ye are not your own? For ye are bought with a price: therefore glorify God in your body, and in your spirit, which are God's" (I Corinthians 6:19-20).* It is easy to forget that we belong to Him. The greatest of all prices was paid for each of us. The **substance** that was given to each servant belonged to the master. Everything that is delivered into our hands is a gift from God! *"For who maketh thee to differ from another? and what hast thou that thou didst not receive? now if thou didst receive it, why dost thou glory, as if thou hadst not received it?" (I Corinthians 4:7) "Every good gift and every perfect gift is from above, and cometh down from the Father of* *lights, with whom is no variableness, neither shadow of turning"* *(James 1:17).* We deserve nothing but the wrath of a Holy God. It is God's grace that causes Him to share His wealth with us!

It is indeed a blessing to be content with what God has given you and where God has placed you. *"But godliness with contentment is great gain" (I Timothy 6:6). "Not that I speak in respect of want: for I have learned, in whatsoever state I am, therewith to be content" (Philippians 4:11).* God called Andrew to be an ordinary, "two talented Christian." It is God that has called you and placed you where you are! Be content!

The Character of the Ordinary Christian

It was God's will that called Andrew to be an ordinary Christian. This station in life would have its limits and its advantages. While there would be certain places Andrew could not go, and things he could not do, he could be a man of character. Character is not determined by what a man has or does not have. Nor is it determined by race or geographical location in the world.

While you may not have the prominence or wealth of this world, you can be a person of character. Character is not something God gives one, but it is something one chooses to be to the glory of God.

Webster defines "character" as a distinctive trait or quality, one's pattern of behavior or personality, moral strength. Andrew's distinctive trait was persistence; his pattern of behavior was purity; and his moral strength can be seen in his proclaiming.

1. Persistence

Andrew occupied a difficult position. Andrew was listed with the group of Peter, James, and John, but he never seemed to enjoy all the privileges that the rest of the group did. While the others went in, Andrew waited outside as the little girl was raised from the dead. When the rest of the group were on the mountain, Andrew was in the valley with the other disciples. It was Peter, James, and John that heard the Lord pray in the garden and saw His sweat turn to great drops of blood. For Andrew, it was like the old adage, "close but not close enough!"

What would you have done in this situation? I know what lots of people do every day! They quit! Their attitude is, "If I cannot be the top dog, I'll take my toys and go home." When one looks at the temperament of James or Peter, it is doubtful that they could have handled playing second fiddle. Though he was a second man, Andrew was persistent.

J.D. Jones said, "Of all the places that test a man's qualities, being in between is the most trying." Andrew, the two talented Christian, was always one step from the bottom and three from the top. Andrew's name is mentioned in twelve verses in the New Testament. One out of every two verses refers to Andrew as Simon Peter's brother. It's almost like Andrew was not even a person apart from Simon Peter. Can you not envision Andrew walking around the marketplace and someone asking, "who are you?" When Andrew gives them his name, they reply, "Oh yes, you're Peter's brother!" Why was Andrew happy being Simon Peter's brother? Because that was the Master's will!

Let it be quickly remembered that it is not position but persistence that God rewards. *"Moreover it is required in stewards, that a man be found faithful" (I Corinthians 4:2).* The word "faithful" means trustworthy, sure, or true. Whether you have five, two, or one talent, it is faithfulness for which the Saviour is looking. It was persistence that caused the five talent servant and the two talent servant to see an increase in talents. It was this persistence that brought glory and honor to their master. You and I can remain true to the Saviour!

2. Purity
If one will take the time to read every place that Andrew's name is mentioned, it becomes evident that nothing negative is said about him. You never hear any dirt about Andrew. While

Andrew is not in the most prominent position, he was pure. Andrew may not be the most popular, but he is pure.

When one begins to look at several of the other apostles, the purity of Andrew's character becomes more apparent. Unlike Judas, Andrew was pure when it came to **money.** Andrew was not consumed with obtaining the wealth and glamour of this world. He knew the value of the eternal over the temporal. Andrew had the right value system! Andrew had not been corrupted by prejudices or hatred. He had remained pure in **mercy.** Unlike Philip, his arms were open to embrace the Greeks that sought out Jesus *(see John 12:20-22).* Andrew's heart was not filled with hatred and the call for the wrath of God like James and John *(see Luke 9:54).* Like the heart of Jesus, Andrew desired to see all men saved. Andrew was pure when it came to **motivation.** He did not have his mother approach the Lord and request a lofty position in the kingdom like the sons of Zebedee *(see Matthew 20:20).* Love for the Lord Jesus Christ fueled the life of Andrew. Lastly, we can see that he was pure in his **mission.** Andrew wanted God's will to be accomplished whether he understood it or not. Unlike Peter, Andrew simply wanted to follow the Lord and not instruct Him *(see Matthew 16:22-23).* Jesus rebuked Peter for having human interests rather than Godly desires. Peter desired his will over the will of the Sovereign.

While Andrew did not appear to be popular or prominent, he was pure when it came to money, mercy, motivation, and his mission. May each of us desire to emulate the example of purity set before us by Andrew.

(3) Proclaiming
It would have been easy for Andrew to become bitter about his station in life! He might have said, "If this is all I get, I'll just keep my mouth shut, and the big three can spread the gospel." This was not the response of Andrew! He just kept telling everyone about his wonderful Lord and Saviour, Jesus Christ.

When the good news of the gospel flooded Andrew's soul, his heart was immediately awakened to the spiritual needs of his brother. While others were busy assessing the bread situation, Andrew was mingling with the crowd. It was there that the problem was solved as Andrew spoke with a little lad. As Philip wrestled with the question of who Jesus came to save, Andrew took the Greeks to the source of eternal life. All Andrew knew to do was to proclaim the good news that Jesus came into the world to save sinners!

The true test of character is not when you're in the lime light but when you're hid from the view of others. Andrew may not have been seen in the room where the little girl was raised from the dead. He was not seen on the mount of transfiguration. Andrew did not appear near the Saviour in the garden, but he remained pure though cloaked by the shadows. How will you act when you think no one can see you? The answer will reveal whether your character is one of purity or that of a pharisee!

The Crop of the Ordinary Christian

In this day of mega-ministries, we are often deceived by the whistles, bells, and trinkets of these religious showmen. It's not in how big the show but what is the substance after all is said and done. When I was a boy, the larger department stores had a big candy counter filled with every kind of candy imaginable. I would pick up soft drink bottles on the school grounds and return them to the local market for money. I would save the change I received until I had enough to buy some candy. One day, I got my accumulated wealth together and headed for town. All I could see was that bag of candy I was going to purchase. When I arrived, I walked around the counter several times, as this was a monumental decision. I could get the maple candy that I knew I liked, or there was this new brand. The new brand was individually wrapped, and you received at least twice as much candy for your money. I went for the new and improved. As I left the store, I opened the first piece. To my surprise, it was nothing more than a large marshmallow. I had spent all my money and had no real substance to show for it.

While there was not a lot of show, there was a lot of substance to Andrew's life. Andrew was raising a crop for the glory of God. He may not have been seen numbered with those at the big events, but his purity, persistence, and proclaiming was yielding fruit. *"He that goeth forth and weepeth, bearing precious seed, shall doubtless come again with rejoicing, bringing his sheaves with him" (Psalm 126:6).* Andrew may have been walking behind a horse pulling a single plow rather than driving some large diesel tractor, but one cannot dispute the quality and quantity of his crop.

When we look at Andrew's crop, I want us to view it from two perspectives; who he enlisted, and who he assisted.

(1) Who He Enlisted
Andrew and another one of John the Baptist's disciples are there that momentous day when John said, *"Behold the Lamb of God" (John 1:36).* Their hearts were afire with an inquiring spirit. Could this be the one they had waited for so long? The next day, Andrew returned with the other disciples, and they listened as Jesus spoke. Never had a man spoken like this man. Driven by the desire to know more, they followed Jesus. Jesus turned and said to them, *"What seek Ye?" (John 1:38)* They replied, *"Rabbi, where dwellest thou?"* In response to His invitation, they spent the entire day with Him. Their eyes could not believe what they saw, neither their ears believe what they heard. Of a truth, this was the Messiah! The discovery was too wonderful to keep to oneself; others must be told. With that, Andrew went forth sowing the seed of the good news to others. Andrew's crop, or harvest, consisted of :

(a) a Brother - *John 1:40-41*
As hard as it was to believe, the one he had heard about as a little child, and the one spoken of in the Scriptures, He had

come. There, before his eyes, was the deliverer. Andrew knew the very person he wanted to break the news to first. It was Simon Peter, his own brother. Being in the same family and in the same business, Andrew and Peter had shared a lot of things. But, this would be the greatest!

I can remember the morning the Lord saved me. It was Easter Sunday morning. The Lord had been dealing with me for a little while, and that morning I went forward to accept God's free gift of eternal life. After some folks had prayed with me, I confirmed that Christ had indeed saved me and arose from the altar. What a blessing, not only had God saved me, but my brother was there on the altar receiving Christ as his Saviour. We had shared the same earthly father, and now, we had the same Heavenly Father.

Have you shared the good news with your family that Jesus came to seek and to save lost sinners? While I did not have the privilege of leading my brother to the Lord, it was a blessing to be there when it happened. Why should we expect others to witness to our family members if we won't? Andrew had gotten hold of something too good to keep to himself; he had to tell Peter. If Jesus is as good as we say He is, and He is, why aren't we telling anyone, especially those we say we love?

(b) a Boy - *John 6:8-9*
There, on the green slopes above the sea of Galilee, an extreme situation had arisen. A multitude of people had followed the Lord and had not eaten all day. Jesus commanded the disciples to feed the people *(Matthew 14:16)*. While the subject upon most of the disciples lips was the expense of bread, and the absence of bread, this was not the case with Andrew. The topic of discussion with Andrew was *"the bread of life" (John 6:35).* While passing among the crowd, Andrew spoke to everyone about the Saviour. Andrew even spent time with a group that the other disciples apparently neglected. From several events recorded for us in God's Word, it would appear that most of the disciples had little time for children. Yet, it was a lad that

Andrew brought to Jesus.

Mark records for us an event where people were bringing their children to Christ, and the disciples were rebuking the people for it. What was our Lord's response? *"But when Jesus saw it, he was much displeased" (Mark 10:14).* The Lord had a special love for children and emphasized the need to reach them with the gospel. Listen to His words, *"Take heed that ye despise not one of these little ones; for I say unto you, That in heaven their angels do always behold the face of my Father which is in heaven. For the Son of man is come to save that which was lost" (Matthew 18:10-11).* Are we guilty of neglecting the children? So many of our children's ministries are set up to meet their social needs and not their spiritual needs! We introduce them to games and not the gospel. The central theme of the youth meeting is the party and not the preaching. May our love for the children and Christ cause us to give ourselves to the ultimate purpose of introducing little ones to the Saviour.

Andrew found the answer to the problem while telling a young lad about the Lord Jesus Christ. The lad was not only convinced to give his life to the Lord but even his lunch. Salvation is giving God it all!

(c) a Barbarian - *John 12:20-22*
When Philip did not know what to do with the Greeks, why did he come to Andrew? Because Andrew knew what to do with all sinners. Get them to Jesus as fast as you can! While we do not like to admit it, each of us are influenced by our prejudices. We all have a group of individuals that we think are outside the boundaries of salvation. These individuals may find themselves on our list of barbarians because of their racial background, political views, social status, cultural background, or fashion choices.

Sometimes it is not the fact that God cannot save them, we don't want God to save them. Was this not the attitude of Jonah?

Jonah knew if he preached to the folks at Nineveh and they showed any kind of repentance, God would be merciful. *"O LORD, was not this my saying, when I was yet in my country? Therefore I fled before unto Tarshish: for I knew that thou art a gracious God, and merciful, slow to anger, and of great kindness, and repentest thee of the evil . . ." (Jonah 4:2b).* Jonah did not want God to be merciful to anyone but Israel. Who is it that you would not have God to save?

While others are trying to decide who needs and does not need to be saved, Andrew is carrying them to God. One never knows just who that individual is and what they may accomplish for God if saved. Tradition suggests that Dr. Luke was one of the Greeks Andrew brought to Jesus. If this be the case, Andrew's crop is still coming in! In his book, "The Twelve," Leslie Flynn tells this story; "Peter Joshua, an unemployed actor, slept in alleys at night and accepted handouts by day. One evening in London's Hyde Park, he saw a Salvation Army girl stand up as if to read poetry. Wanting to give her support, he found himself her only audience. Instead of reading poetry, she began to sing. It was a hymn that showed the worthlessness of the world compared to the glories of Christ. Looking straight in the face of Joshua, she quoted several Bible verses, then turned and went her way. Right then, Joshua received Christ. Years later, there was a sunrise service in Chicago's Soldiers Field. There were 70,000 people in that great Resurrection Celebration. The featured speaker was Dr. Peter Joshua, pastor and evangelist. If that little Salvation Army girl could have only seen him now!"

(2) Who He Assisted

Andrew knew something that many of us have forgotten. *"For we are labourers together with God" (I Corinthians 3:9). "Go ye therefore . . . and, lo, I am with you alway, even unto the end of the world. Amen" (Matthew 28:19-20).* Andrew did not see himself as laboring alone but perceived himself as a co-laborer with the Lord Jesus Christ. Andrew was assisting God in the harvest! Having the right partner, Andrew was able to:

(a) Enlarge the Ministry - *John 1:40-41*

When Andrew ran to tell his brother about Jesus, he did not know to what capacity God would use Simon Peter. While Andrew would not stand and preach to thousands, the brother he brought to Christ would. While Andrew would not be the penman of inspired portions of the Word of God, his convert would. The ministry was enlarged, not so much by Andrew personally, but by Andrew's personal work when he told his brother about the Christ. While everyone knows D.L. Moody, few know the Sunday School teacher that made a personal visit to a shoe shop for the express purpose of witnessing to young Moody. The Prince of Preachers, Charles H. Spurgeon, is known throughout the world, but what was the man's name whom God used to awaken young Spurgeon's heart to its spiritual need?

While we may be ordinary, the person to whom we give the gospel may be extraordinary. One can never be sure to what extent the ministry is being enlarged by our faithfulness to personal work!

(b) Execute a Miracle - *John 6:8-12*

You never read where Andrew raised someone from the dead. Andrew never walked on the water or caused water to be turned to wine. While Andrew never personally performed a miracle, he did help execute one when he brought the lad to the Saviour. Andrew's personal work helped to place at Jesus' disposal the things needed to perform a miracle. You and I may never perform miracles, but we can help execute a miracle. Each of us can be part of the miracle of the new birth by faithfully giving forth the gospel of Jesus Christ. We can see people translated out of the kingdom of darkness into the kingdom of God's dear Son. When the believer prays in accordance with God's will, all the powers of heaven are set in motion to work in miraculous ways. We can make available to God a vessel through which He can do the miraculous.

(c) Expose the Master and His Mercy - *John 12:20-22*

When Andrew took the Greeks to Jesus, he exposed to the world the goodness, grace, and mercies of our great God and Saviour, Jesus Christ. Tradition tells us that Dr. Luke was one of the Greeks Andrew took to Jesus. Andrew's personal work did not end in Jerusalem but has covered the entire world through the writings of Dr. Luke. Andrew's witness did not die when he did because the inspired writing of Luke's gospel are still being read today. If each of us will be faithful to God's call to tell others, there is no telling to what extent we will expose the world to our Lord and Saviour, Jesus Christ.

Andrew worked from his **Family** to the **Foreigner**. *"But ye shall receive power, after that the Holy Ghost is come upon you: and ye shall be witnesses unto me both in Jerusalem, and in all Judaea, and in Samaria, and unto the uttermost part of the earth" (Acts 1:8).* Andrew had a crop that honored God and will generate rewards in heaven. Everyone of us are raising a crop. When the day of harvest has past, what will abound unto your account?

Andrew was that two talent Christian that had a dream of doing something for God. It reminds me of an account in the life of King David when he wanted to build a house for God. As Nathan and David fellowshipped one evening in the palace, David looked out the window and saw the drab colored tent that made up the House of God. David told Nathan, "I'm going to build God a house." David had a desire to do something to honor his God and show the Lord how much he loved Him. God's response to David's heart's desire was, *"Thou shalt not build me an house to dwell in" (I Chronicles 17:4).* This was not something David wanted to do for David but something David wanted to do for God! God said "No!" With the negative, God spoke of several positives. While David was not permitted to do for God, God was going to do for David. God was going to give David rest from all his enemies, let David's son build the house, and establish the throne of David. But, in the midst of it all, God had these words for David, *"Whereas it was in thine heart to build an house unto my name, thou didst well that it was in thine heart"* (I Kings 8:18).

While God was interested in what was in David's hands, He was more interested in what was in his heart! **Your greatest blessing from God may be two talents coupled with a desire for five!** For, you see, while the man with two talents never became a five, he did become a four! Maybe the most important question is not "How many talents do I have?", but "What's in my heart?"

Chapter Four

James, the Self-Centered Christian

Mark 1:19-20 And when he had gone a little farther thence, he saw James the son of Zebedee, and John his brother, who also were in the ship mending their nets. And straightway he called them: and they left their father Zebedee in the ship with the hired servants, and went after him."

Upon coming into Galilee, Jesus began to preach the gospel of the kingdom of God. As He walked by the sea of Galilee, He saw two brothers, Andrew and Peter, casting their net into the sea. The Lord called them to follow Him. When He had gone a little farther, the Lord saw two brothers, James and John, mending their nets. He commanded them to leave their nets and follow Him. James and John left all to follow our Lord. J.D. Jones tells us that James and John were drawn from a higher social class than the rest of the apostles. It is evident from the gospels that their father, Zebedee, was a prosperous man in the fishing business. Zebedee had servants as well as sons to help him in the business of fishing. Because of their social status, the family had connections with some of the leading families in Jerusalem.

Upon accepting the call to follow the Lord, James was given a place of prominence. James was not just an apostle, but he had been chosen by the Lord to be part of the inner circle. The inner circle was comprised of Peter, James and John. This inner circle had the opportunity of getting to know the Lord Jesus in a greater capacity than the others. I am not sure they took advantage of the privilege, but it was theirs for the taking. As a member of the inner circle, James could have known the **power**

of God. When others were not permitted behind closed doors, he saw individuals healed and people raised from the dead *(see Mark 5:36-43)*. Jesus commanded the others to remain at the foot of the mountain while He, Peter, James, and John went into the mount. It was there that James saw the **person of God**. With his eyes, James saw the raiment of Christ shine as God manifested His glory. With his ears, James heard the voice of God as it told of Christ's preeminence. As the disciples entered the garden, only three were permitted to enter into its heart. There James saw the **passion of God** as the Lord's sweat became great drops of blood. It requires little gray matter to perceive that James occupied a special position.

Yet, opportunity and privilege is no guarantee that one will be totally committed to or be right with God. You may have been born in America where we are privileged to have religious liberties. You can worship where, when, and how you please. You could have been raised in a pastor's home, or possibly your parents were very active in the church. You may have been educated in a Christian school. All these things are privileges and opportunities, they are not guarantees that you are in a right relationship with God! While James may have enjoyed the opportunity of being special, James was self-centered. As a matter of fact, sometimes special privilege is a deterrent to spiritual growth. Paul knew this truth when he spoke of the thorn in the flesh. Paul had enjoyed an abundance of revelations *(see II Corinthians 12:7)*, and sometimes privilege gives way to the element of pride. The thorn kept Paul from being filled with pride and becoming self-centered.

Each of us would like to perceive ourselves as kind and considerate of others. While we sometimes fail to admit or recognize our self-centered spirit, there is one that has complete knowledge of that evil disposition. As Jesus' disciples gathered about Him, He chose twelve and ordained that they should be with Him *(see Mark 3:8-14)*. In *Mark 3:16-19*, the twelve are listed for us. When James and John are mentioned, the following statement is made, *"he surnamed them Boanerges, which is, The sons of thunder."* J.D. Jones tells us that the name implies, a man of stormy and tempestuous zeal, not a man of eloquence." While the two brothers may not have been aware of this self-centered spirit, the Lord Jesus knew what was in their heart. Let each one of us remember that the Lord knows our disposition as well. Just like James, we too try to hide our exaltation of self behind the pious front of defending the honor and ministry of Christ. When this happens, we are only fooling ourselves. He knows it all!

There are three specific events in which the self-centeredness of James can be readily seen: *Mark 9:38, Mark 10:35, & Luke 9:54.* As we look at James, the self-centered Christian, may he serve as a rebuke to the wickedness of our own hearts. Note three areas with me.

The Self-Centered and His Ego
If one is going to understand and combat being self-centered, there is one area that must be investigated. There must be an honest evaluation of the ego. Webster defines the term as the self; the individual as aware of himself. It does not take long to realize that James had a rather large ego. James was a self-centered individual because he had an over evaluated opinion of himself. A psychologist might describe James as having a large or inflated ego, but the Word of God calls it pride.

Part of James' problem was that he had over-valued himself while under-valuing those about him. Have you been guilty of this kind of thinking? I know it is hard to admit, but many times we think that God couldn't operate without us; that church wouldn't be what it is if it were not for my ministry! They wouldn't have had a Christmas play if I hadn't done all the work! I keep the whole soprano section in tune; they couldn't sing a lick if I weren't there! There wouldn't have been any preaching at that meeting if I hadn't been there! While we may not have vocalized these types of remarks, have they not been harbored in our hearts? God calls this type of spirit pride!

Pride will not permit the individual to see the true value of others. Pride caused James to under-value those about him. He perceived that everyone and everything was there to serve him. Why would James come to this conclusion? Simple! James was the most important person there. From the Scriptures, we can see three things that James under-valued.

1. The Service of Others - *Mark 9:38*
Jesus had made his way to Capernaum with His disciples. When they had entered into a house, Jesus asked them what it was that they had disputed over. None of the disciples would answer the Lord's question. Because our Lord knows the thoughts and intents of the heart, He knew the dispute was over who would be the greatest. To combat this spirit of pride or self-centeredness, Jesus called for the disciples to gather about Him. Using a little child, Jesus taught a lesson on humility. Smitten in his heart, John remembered an event where he and some of the other disciples had rebuked a man for casting out devils. James was most likely right there in the thick of things. John's words were, *"we saw one casting out devils in thy name, and he followeth not us: and we forbad him, because he followeth not us."* Note the repetitive pronouns we and us. In just about every case, John and James were inseparable.

The disciples saw this man casting out devils, and they forbad him. The word means to prevent by word or act, to hinder or keep from. James and the others kept this individual from serving the Lord. What generated this self-centered spirit among the disciples in this event?

The disciples might have became upset because this nobody had just accomplished what they had failed to achieve. In *Mark 9:28,* the disciples asked the Lord why they had been unable to cast out the evil spirit. Here was an individual with no prominent position, nor the spiritual education as the hand picked apostles had, and he was performing where they have failed. Don't things like that just eat you alive? Here you are, you have worked and fought to get to the place of honor and some nobody steals all your thunder. There is no way God could be in that!

The individual did not fly the same flag they did. To put it into our spiritual lingo, he was not in their camp. As far as the disciples were concerned, God could not use anyone unless that individual or group fit into their mold. The only trouble with that theology is that it was not true. I must readily admit that it is difficult for me to deal with the fact that God uses people and groups that I would not use. If I am not very careful, I will inflate the value of my ministry and minimize the ministry of others. Jesus told the disciples to leave him alone and not to hinder his service. Two examples of this truth can be seen in the life of Moses and in the life of the Apostle Paul *(see Numbers 11:29 & Philippians 1:18)*. One being in reference to prophesying and the other preaching.

James' pride and self-centered spirit caused him to under-value the service of others. May we not be guilty of doing the same. All of God's people are important to the work of God.

2. The Sacrifice of Self - *Mark 10:37*
James and John approached the Lord with a request. *"We would that thou shouldest do for us whatsoever we shall desire. . . Grant unto us that we may sit, one on thy right hand, and the other on thy left hand, in thy glory" Mark 10:35&37.* One writer said, they requested preeminence, proximity, and power. James desired to elevate self not execute self. James was filled with earthly ambition at the expense of spiritual discernment!

Like so many of us, these men wanted a crown without a cross. They did not understand that all the things they desired were achieved through sacrifice. Their thoughts were, why shouldn't we occupy the place of preeminence; we were one of the first to be chosen. We were part of the inner circle, and we have family ties, cousins no less. We have breeding and social prominence. Who is more deserving of those two seats than us? While it may not be a throne by the Saviour's side, it may be a place on the deacon board or some special committee you see yourself worthy of occupying. It may be the prominent place on the program, when the crowds are the largest, that your talents would be best suited. Surely, you're the only person they would consider for the lead role in the church play.

Whatever happened to following the example of our Lord and taking the place of a servant? *"He riseth from supper, and laid aside his garments; and took a towel, and girded himself. After that he poureth water into a basin, and began to wash the disciples' feet, and to wipe them with the towel wherewith he was girded" (John 13:4-5).* What about the words of the Apostle Paul, *"I beseech you therefore, brethren, by the mercies of God, that ye present your bodies a living sacrifice, holy, acceptable unto God, which is your reasonable service?" Romans 12:1* Have you seen the importance of sacrifice in the Christian life?

3. The Soul of Sinners - *Luke 9:54*
Jesus knew that all things were ready. In a short while, he would offer Himself for the sins of the world. The final journey to Jerusalem included passing through Samaria *(see Luke 9:52).* In the process of journeying to Jerusalem, there would be certain physical needs, and messengers were sent ahead to make ready for the group. At a particular Samaritan village, they refused to welcome the Lord and His company. When James and John got wind of this inhospitable act, their response was, *"wilt thou that we command fire to come down from heaven, and consume them, even as Elias did?" Luke 9:54* Because these people had rejected this large company of people, James wanted to execute them all. James' thoughts were, I'll just do what Elijah did; I'll call fire out of heaven and destroy every living soul.

What may have appeared as righteous indignation was most likely a response to having his feelings hurt. Just who do these folks think they were rejecting the Lord, and His twelve personal, hand picked, sacrificial and dedicated servants to the most high God?

James placed more value on his religious position and the party he was with than the eternal soul of those in the village. While it may not have been a vocal response, his actions were saying, these folks don't deserve to be saved. They are only fit for hell. Jesus rebuked the two brothers with these words, *"For the Son of man is not come to destroy men's lives, but to save them."* *Luke 9:56*

What could cause James to undervalue the worth of a single soul? James may have had a hard time dealing with their **sin**. Because of our immaturity and ignorance, we categorize sin as big and little. These Samaritans had not committed a little sin; this was a big sin. When someone is guilty of big sins, we assume that they do not deserve God's love and mercy. This may shock you, but I agree totally, one hundred percent. These people do not deserve to be saved but neither does anyone else. It is not the fact that you have little sins and I have big sins, it is the fact that we have sinned. There are none righteous, and there are none that are deserving of God's mercy and grace! Each of us must remember that God can and will forgive people you and I won't. There are some lifestyles with which I have a great deal of trouble. I find it hard to love the sinner because of their sin. Yet, these same people are not beyond the boundaries of His grace! Besides, it is not our forgiveness that they need, it is His!

James may have wanted to execute them because of their **sect.** These people were not Jews but Samaritans. The Jews were God's chosen people, and they had no dealing with those half breeds. The Samaritan people were a mix of Jew and gentile dog. Why would God want to save the likes of them? Is this not the attitude of Jonah when God commissioned him to go to Nineveh? While we do not like to admit it, our determination of who is worth saving and who isn't is tainted with personal prejudices. God's love is not tainted with prejudice because He has put all men into the same class, *"There is none righteous, no, not one" Romans 3:10.*

James' self-centered spirit was generated by pride. He had placed the value of his person, position, and plans above everything else. This had caused James to undervalue the service of others, the sacrifice of self, and the soul of sinners. It is only when we have a proper view of self that we can combat becoming self-centered.

The Self-Centered and His Education
When one studies the life of James and his tendency to be self-centered, it becomes obvious that he needed to be educated in at least three areas. There were certain principles and truths in the Word of God that would have served to destroy this bad spirit in James' life. What is true for James is true for all! If each of us would expose ourselves to more of the teaching and preaching of God's Word, we would find ourselves more like God's perfect Son, the Lord Jesus.

1. The Place They Serve - *Mark 9:38*
When John and the other disciples began to rebuke this individual for casting out devils, they were minimizing his service for the Lord Jesus. The disciples stopped him because they did not see the value of what he was doing for the Lord. We, as well as the disciples, need to remember that it is God that chooses where a person serves and how they are to serve. *"But now hath God set the members every one of them in the body, as it hath pleased him" I Corinthians 12:18.* It was not James' responsibility to determine where and how this individual was to serve God. James needed to remember that there are no big and little positions in the body. There are no insignificant members in the body, but all are important and needed. When we begin to sit in judgment of another believer, may we remember these words, *"Who art thou that judgest another man's servant? to his own master he standeth or falleth" Romans 14:4.* If we are not

careful, we begin to elevate ourselves to lofty position at the expense of unity within the body of Christ. This is what happened among the believers at Corinth. Paul responded by saying, *"Who then is Paul, and who is Apollos, but ministers by whom ye believed, even as the Lord gave to every man?"* I Corinthians 3:5 We tend to be less self-centered when we remember that each of us have been placed in the body as pleasing unto the Lord. All members are needed and important!

2. The Price They Pay - *Mark 10:39*

When James and John asked for the two seats on either side of the Lord Jesus, Jesus responded with a question, *"can ye drink of the cup that I drink of? and be baptized with the baptism that I am baptized with?" Mark 9:38* Their answer reveals the shallowness of their understanding. They said, *"We can."* The cup our Lord spoke of was one of bitterness as He tasted death for all men. His reference to baptism was that of being immersed in trouble and sorrow. This reference to baptism pictures for us a similar scene, that of Jonah in the fish's belly. *"The waters compassed me about, even to the soul: the depth closed me round about, the weeds were wrapped about my head" Jonah 2:5.* Jesus wanted to know if James was ready for that kind of life. After the affirmative answer, Jesus said, *"Ye shall indeed drink of the cup that I drink of; and with the baptism that I am baptized withal shall ye be baptized."* James was then educated in the suffering associated with the Christian life. *"Yea, and all that will live godly in Christ Jesus shall suffer persecution" II Timothy 3:12.* There is a price to be paid for occupying a place closest to the Saviour. In *John 15*, Jesus told the disciples to expect to receive the same treatment from the world that He received. How did the world react to the Son of God? They crucified Him! Yes, there is a crown to be worn and a heaven to enjoy, but before we get there, there is a cross to bear and hatred to endure. *"But the God of all grace, who hath called us unto his eternal glory by Christ Jesus, after that ye have suffered a while, make you perfect, stablish, strengthen, settle you" I Peter 5:10.*

3. The Passion They Need - *Luke 9:55*

With the thoughts of vindication in their minds, James and John asked for an execution fire from heaven. In His rebuke, the Lord not only told of the purpose for His coming, *"to save them,"* but He revealed a passion. It was a passion that neither of these two men possessed. Jesus had a love for the souls of men, and these men did not share that passion. Jesus said, *"Ye know not what manner of spirit ye are of."* Jesus wanted James to know that he did not share the same type of spirit that God had when it came to lost humanity. James encouraged destruction while God wanted to provide deliverance. James was only thinking of self, and the Lord was pondering sacrifice. It is only when we become educated to the value of a soul that we will become less self-centered and more conscious of the sinner's need. May we follow the admonition of our Lord when He said, *"Lift up your eyes, and **look on the** fields; for they are white already to harvest" John 4:35.*

The Self-Centered and His Effect

When one looks at the self-centeredness of James, it would be nice to say that this type of spirit affected no one but James. Yet, this is not true! A self-centered Christian has an effect on all those about him. James affected other **servants**, **saints** of God, and **sinners** that needed a witness. James' self-centered spirit was something that each of us should consider repulsive and undesirable in our own personal lives. Each of us must remember that we do have an effect on those about us. *"For none of us liveth to himself, and no man dieth to himself" Romans 14:7.* We can see three negative effects of James' self-centered spirit.

1. Hindered Others

When James and John found this individual casting out devils, they said "we rebuked him." The word they used means to prevent, to hinder, or to keep from. They hindered the ministry and service this person was doing for God. How many times has our self-centered, arrogant spirit hindered others from serving the Lord? A critical spirit could have prevented the woman from anointing the body of Jesus. Jesus said, *"She hath done what she could" Mark 14:8.* May each of us purpose not to barricade the way to serving God, but may each of us bridge the gaps with encouragement and helps so others may do what they can for His glory. Let it be remembered that when we hinder others from serving the Lord, we have hindered the work of God, thus hindering God.

2. Harmed the Body

James and John confronted the Lord with the request for the place of preeminence. It was a constant point of contention among the disciples on who was to be the greatest. When word got to the others of the request, it just added fuel to the fire. *"And when the ten heard it, they began to be much displeased with James and John" Mark 10:41.* The word displeased means greatly afflicted, to be moved with indignation. James' self-centered spirit harmed the body of Christ. If there is one thing God does not want in the body, it is division. Listen to the words of Paul to the believers at Corinth, *"That there should be no schism in the body; but that the members should have the same care one for another" I Corinthians 12:25.* Does your spirit promote unity or does it encourage division within the body of Christ?

3. Hatred it Generated

At the rejection of the Samaritan people, James and John responded with, *"Lord, wilt thou that we command fire to come down from heaven, and consume them, even as Elias did?" Luke 9:54* I do not know if word got back to those in the village about James' and John's actions, but if it did, what kind of reaction would it have generated in those Samaritan people? Being worldly people, the Samaritan people would most likely have responded to the hatred of James and John with hatred themselves. Knowing the heart of James and John, how receptive to the gospel do you think these folks would be now? Jesus tells us in *Matthew 5* that we are to love our enemy. If someone acts toward us in an evil manner, we are to respond with love and kindness. Paul tells us that we are to combat evil with good. *"Therefore if thine enemy hunger, feed him; if he thirst, give him drink: for in so doing thou shalt heap coals of fire on his head. Be not overcome of evil, but overcome evil with good" Romans 12:21-22.* A self-centered spirit only generates hatred in the lives of others.

As one continues to study the life of James, it is exciting to report the death of that self-centered spirit in James' life. We see harmony in the body as James and the other disciples gathered in the upper room *(see Acts 1:13)*. There was the spirit of humility as James became the brother of John *(see Acts 12:2)*. Because of James' leadership role and influence, James was martyred fourteen years after the crucifixion for the cause of Christ *"And he killed James the brother of John with the sword" Acts 12:2.* Gaston Foote said, "He went from a man of selfish desire for physical power, a desire to dominate, an aspiration for leadership, to a man of devotion and convictions that made him the first among the disciples to sacrifice his life for his Lord." There is an old legend which says that one of those who bore false witness against James before Herod, was so overcome by the Apostle's earnestness and zeal and holy courage, that he then and there confessed himself a Christian and was carried off with James to execution. On the way to the block, he longed for forgiveness of the Apostle. Giving him the kiss of forgiveness and saying peace be unto you, James and his latest convert died together. May the life of James encourage us to turn from a self-centered spirit to one of sweetness and humility.

Chapter Five

John, the Loving Christian

John 21:20-24 "Then Peter, turning about, seeth the disciple whom Jesus loved following; which also leaned on his breast at supper, and said, Lord, which is he that betrayeth thee? Peter seeing him saith to Jesus, Lord, and what shall this man do? Jesus saith unto him, If I will that he tarry till I come, what is that to thee? follow thou me. Then went this saying abroad among the brethren, that that disciple should not die: yet Jesus said not unto him, He shall not die; but, If I will that he tarry till I come, what is that to thee? This is the disciple which testifieth of these things, and wrote these things: and we know that his testimony is true."

When speaking of John, one writer said, "John is the greatest of all the apostles in the opinion of many. He occupied an extensive place in the New Testament, an important place, and a unique place." J.D. Jones points out that many Bible personalities have a great legacy. "Enoch, he walked with God. Moses, he talked with God. David, he was the man after God's own heart. But, one of the greatest was said of John, the disciple whom Jesus loved." John was chosen to be one of the twelve and then chosen to be in the inner circle, but in the end, he was in a class all by himself. While John was referred to three times as that other or another, five times he had the honor of being referred to as the disciple whom Jesus loved.

It is accepted by most that John was the youngest of the apostles. Most feel John was under twenty and probably a teenager when he began to follow Jesus. It became apparent that John was very attached to Simon Peter. Prior to responding to the call of Christ in *Mark 1:19,* John was one of Simon's partners in the fishing business *(see Luke 5:10).* But, this attachment grew only stronger as both John and Simon left all to follow Christ. Whether it was the impressionable character of Simon or some other trait, John took his place alongside Peter. It was Peter and John that prepared the last Passover feast for Jesus *(see Luke 22:8).* In the first nine chapters of the book of *Acts,* it was Peter with John at his side. While they were partners in the fishing business, their greatest endeavor was their partnership in the task of being fishers of men.

John was a Galilean and was the brother of James. Their parents were Zebedee and Salome. Salome was the sister of Mary the mother of Jesus. John was not only tied to Jesus through family but by faith which he exhibited in his willingness to leave all and follow Christ.

This youthful apostle was not without his problems. In *Mark 9,* John rebuked an individual for casting out devils in Jesus' name because the individual would not follow him. In an anxious moment, John desired to call fire down out of heaven and destroy a village of Samaritans that would not receive Christ *(see Luke 9:54).* We are allowed to see John's ambitious spirit when he and his brother asked for the honor of occupying the thrones on either side of Jesus in the kingdom *(see Mark 10:37).* While these incidents revealed John's human flaws, the overshadowing element in his character was his heart! John had a heart for God. John was the disciple whom Jesus loved. William A. McIntyre said, "The name John means one whom Jehovah loveth or favored of Jehovah. J. Golder Burns asked this question, "If John's proudest boast was to be the special object of Christ's love, what is our proudest boast?"

What does it mean to be the disciple whom Jesus loved? Gaston Foote said, "Jesus had no 'teacher's pet,' but the tender, demonstrably affectionate nature of John drew from Jesus a demonstrative response." It was not so much that John was

Jesus' first choice, but Jesus was John's first choice! *"I love them that love me; and those that seek me early shall find me" Proverbs 8:17.* John positioned himself so that he could experience the fullness of the love of Christ. Love will open the door of opportunity that monetary means, social status, and educational excellence can never approach. This love relationship between John and the Lord Jesus gave way to momentous opportunities.

The Communion of Love - *vs.20*

Have you ever heard someone make this statement, I don't feel comfortable around that person? Love destroys those kinds of feelings. True love does not repel or hold at a distance, but it bids one to draw near. If there was one place that John felt comfortable, it was near to Jesus. The reference to John leaning on the breast of our Lord was the position he took at the Passover feast *(see John 13:25).*

People are creatures of habit. I know when I was growing up at home, everyone sat in the same place at meal time. If someone got in my place, I set up a howl! This principle is true at church. I noticed it when I pastored, and I have noticed it as I travel to different churches in evangelism. People like to sit in the same place. We are not told for certain, and I cannot prove it, but I believe that John occupied the place closest to the Lord on a regular basis. The Oriental custom was to lie with the left arm on the cushion and the right free to partake of the banquet, so that the head of one guest would frequently reach back to the girdle of the other.

Love for the Lord compelled John to get as close as he could to the Saviour. In any relationship, the quality of love is proportional to the desire to be near. When a young man and young lady become interested in one another, their desire to be near each other intensifies. If the relationship continues to grow, soon you will not see one without the other. Why? Love demands a state of communion! They get married so they can be together all the time. Years pass and one is taken in death. The one remaining is overheard saying, I don't think I can live without them. Love is not willing to give up that close and personal communion.

If you want to evaluate the quality of your love for the Lord, just find out how much time you want to spend with Him, and you will have your answer. If you find yourself missing services, neglecting the Word of God, and doing very little praying, it is a good sign that your love for Him has grown cold.

Why do you always find John wanting to be close to Jesus? What caused him to go to the High Priest's house the night Jesus was taken? What caused him to be near the cross at the Lord's crucifixion? Why did he out run the other disciple to the tomb? Love! Love! Love! Love will accept no distance to come between it and the object of its affection. How far away are you?

The Communication of Love - *vs.20*

When the disciples gathered for the final Passover feast before our Lord's death, John positioned himself in that special place nearest Jesus. It became evident that Jesus was troubled in His spirit and He had to tell those closest to Him what was bothering Him. *"Verily, verily, I say unto you, that one of you shall betray me" John 13:21.* With the exception of Judas, all the disciples were taken back by such a statement. They began to look one on another and wonder of whom He spake. It was then that Peter motioned to John. Peter was encouraging John to ask Jesus to identify the traitor. Lying upon the breast of our Lord, John turns to the Saviour saying, *"Lord, who is it?" John 13:25* Why had Peter not asked for himself? If there was one thing that was common knowledge to all those present, it was that Peter never had any trouble working his mouth. He may have had trouble stopping but never starting when it came to talking. So, why did he want John to ask? Occupying a special place yields special privileges. One of which is communication!

Love has no secrets. The greatest secret treasures of the heart are openly shared between lovers. If there was one person that could get an answer to who the betrayer was, it was *"the disciple whom Jesus loved."* The greater the love, the greater the communication! When no one could find the secret to the strength of Samson, the lords of the Philistines turned to a woman named Delilah. On several occasions she asked him what the secret of his strength was, and he would not tell her the truth. Delilah said, *"How canst thou say, I love thee, when thine heart is not with me? thou hast mocked me these three times, and hast not told me wherein thy great strength lieth" Judges 16:15.* Love will not deceive or lie to the object of its affection. Love must communicate, *"he told her all his heart, and said unto her, There hath not come a razor upon mine head; for I have been a Nazarite unto God from my mother's womb: if I be shaven, then my strength will go from me, and I shall become weak, and be like any other man. And when Delilah saw that he had told her all his heart, she sent and called for the lords of the Philistines" Judges 16:17-18.*

If you want to know the quality of your love for Christ, just check the level of communication. Do you talk with Him regularly about everything? Is there anything you are trying to hide from Him? We are encouraged to come to the Lord and speak openly to Him. *"Let us therefore come boldly unto the throne of grace, that we may obtain mercy, and find grace to help in time of need" Hebrews 4:16.*

The Commission of Love - *vs.21*

The morning was still fresh as the disciples gathered about the fire. Jesus began to pass each of them some bread and fish. When they were finishing the last of the breakfast, Jesus broke the silence with a question, *"Simon, son of Jonas, lovest thou me more than these?" John 21:15* Three times Jesus questioned the love of Simon Peter. With each affirmative answer, Peter was given a command to serve, *"Feed my lambs", "Feed my sheep", "Feed my sheep" (see John 21:15,16,17).* By making these demands on Simon Peter, Jesus was revealing a great truth about love. Love serves the object it loves! If Peter was truly in love with the Lord, he would render service to the Lord. If you are truly in love with the Lord, you will serve Him!

There are two areas that need to be considered when one looks at the commission of love. First, it is a **personal** commission. Peter had been given the command to feed three times. In response to Jesus' command, Peter said, *"what shall this man do?" (see John 21:21)* Peter did not need to worry how John was going to serve the Lord, and John did not need to worry how Peter was going to serve the Lord. Love is not concerned with what someone else is doing, but how can I express my love to the Lord by the means of service?

There is the **particular** commission of love. Love does not serve the object of its affection where it wants to serve. Love will seek out the will and the desires of its object and serve. When Jesus was on the cross, one of the last things he did was to search out one to care for His mother. Jesus turned to John and said, *"Behold thy mother!" (see John 19:27)* What was John's response to the Lord's command? Lord, I don't want to do that, or I had something else in mind. No! *"And from that hour that disciple took her unto his own home" John 19:27.* Love will not be satisfied with just serving the one it loves, but it wants to do those things which are in accordance to the object's will. If I truly love the Lord, I will not only want to serve Him, but I will serve where He wants me to serve.

Are you involved in a personal and a particular service for Christ? Find out what you are giving the most time, talent, and treasures to, and you will know what you love. *"For where your treasure is, there will your heart be also" Matthew 6:21.*

The Consistency of Love - *vs.20*
After the Lord had commanded Peter to feed, He then said, *"Follow me" (see John 21:19).* This was not the first time Peter

was called by God to follow. The first time was by the Sea of Galilee *(see Matthew 4:19)*. As Peter rose from the fireside and began to pursue the Lord, he turned to see the disciple whom Jesus loveth following. It had been over three years since Jesus passed by and called John into His service *(see Matthew 4:21)*. Yet, we have no record of the Lord having to come to John a second time and encourage him to follow. John's love for the Lord made him consistent in his service to the Lord. Listen to what God's Word says about the consistency of love, *"Charity suffereth long"* and *"Charity never faileth" I Corinthians 13:4&8.* Love will not be turned away from the object of its affection.

There was the consistency of a **relationship**. Love will not allow anything to get between them and the one they love. When others had quit and turned back, John's love for the Lord would not allow him to quit. See John as he pursued the Lord into the courtyard of the high priest's house *(see John 18:15-16)*. In the Lord's time of suffering and anguish, who would be there to share that moment with Him but those that loved Him most. One that was nearest to the cross was the disciple whom Jesus loved. Who was the first of the disciples to get to the tomb? *"So they ran both together: and the other disciple did outrun Peter, and came first to the sepulchre" John 20:4.* Love will remain true to the one it loves. How would you describe your relationship to Christ when it comes to consistency?

The consistency of love is characterized by **remembrance**. John's love would not allow him to forget the words, actions, or promises of his love. As one looks closely at the book of *John,* it becomes evident that nearly half of the verses are the words of our Lord. John even remembered things that are not recorded for us in the cannon of Scripture. *"And there are also many other things which Jesus did, the which, if they should be written every one, I suppose that even the world itself could not contain the books that should be written. Amen" John 21:25.* John's writings are given to details others did not include. Only John records the words, *"I thirst"* and *"it is finished" (see John 19)*. Only John tells of the Lord bowing His head and releasing His spirit. It was John that saw the side pierced and tells us of the burial by Nicodemus and Joseph. Everywhere John went and everything John did or saw were just stimuli to provoke the memory. The Lord was ever on the mind and in the heart of John. How much do you think of Him?

The Consciousness of Love - *vs. 7*

The boat tossed gently in the morning light. Having toiled all night, the disciples had not even one fish to show for their efforts. As the shadows gave way to the light, a lone figure appeared on the shore. He cried, *"Children, have ye any meat?" John 21:5* In the midst of their discouragement, the stranger told them to cast their net on the right side. Immediately, they enclosed a multitude of fishes. While the others were preoccupied with the situation, John was interested in the stranger. It took him no time to discern who the lone figure was! *"Therefore that disciple whom Jesus loved saith unto Peter, It is the Lord" John 21:7.* When no one else knew who was near, John knew. Why? Love is always sensitive to the presence of the one it loves.

What a blessing it is to be traveling down the road either coming from or going to a meeting and become conscious of His presence. Just to know that He has drawn near. It may be in the midst of a crowded waiting room at the hospital when all are intent on the seriousness of the moment; it is then that you become aware of another that has come to breathe peace on your troubled soul. What will heighten one's sensitivity to the nearness of the Lord? Love! Love is always looking for any evidence that their love is near.

John was the loving Christian, and this love gave way to privilege. Love will break down all barriers and open doors of opportunity. Love allowed John to gain entrance into a **special place** where there was **communion**, a **speaking place** where there was **communication**, a **serving place** where there was a **commission**, a **steadfast place** where there was **consistency**, and a **sensitive place** where there was a **consciousness** of His presence. One key will open all these doors; it is the key of love. John is remembered for being the disciple whom Jesus loved because Jesus occupied first place in John's heart.

When the Lord spoke to the church of Ephesus, He spoke highly of their works, labours, and patience. Yet, with all the good, there was one overshadowing fact, they had left their first love. God is more interested in your love than He is in your labors. John gave Jesus first place in his heart. This put John in the position to enjoy all the blessings that are associated with love. You too can experience the fullness of God's love! *"Draw nigh to God, and he will draw nigh to you" James 4:8.* Are you moving toward Him?

Chapter Six

Philip, the Limited Christian

"The day following Jesus would go forth into Galilee, and findeth Philip, and saith unto him, Follow me. Now Philip was of Bethsaida, the city of Andrew and Peter. Philip findeth Nathanael, and saith unto him, We have found him, of whom Moses in the law, and the prophets, did write, Jesus of Nazareth, the son of Joseph. And Nathanael said unto him, Can there any good thing come out of Nazareth? Philip saith unto him, Come and see" (John 1:43-46).

Philip was a native of Bethsaida, the city of Andrew and Peter. Nothing is known of his earlier occupation, but it is speculated that he was a fisherman. Like Andrew, he had a Greek name but was probably not of Greek origin.

When the name Philip comes up, most will use terms like level-headed, prudent, or practical. These terms are those associated with wisdom rather than education. Education gives you the facts. Wisdom is the ability to know how and when to use them! It is indeed a blessing to possess this gift of wisdom.

While these are good attributes in their proper place, they are many times just a cloak to hide our shallow faith in Christ. I believe this is the kind of individual Philip was. If Peter could be accused of leaping before he looked, Philip was the individual that looked and wouldn't leap. Philip was a limited Christian. He was not limited by the Saviour but by himself. Philip is not the kind of person that lacked talent, ability, or opportunity. Rather, Philip is one that shackles these privileges so that they cannot be used to their full potential. Philip had everything except the faith

72

to commit everything to the Lord, even the results.

Philip reminds me of a Labrador Retriever I had when I was a boy. I had a passion for duck hunting and decided that I needed a dog to retrieve the game. I bought a pup and began the training process. Jody seemed to possess all the skills and ability needed to make a good hunting dog, that is except one. He did not want to jump into the water. Jody could swim and would swim. He loved to go hunting and would retrieve. But Jody's approach to the water was to wade in a little at a time, testing before committing to it. He had all the skills and ability, but not the confidence to use them.

I know in my own personal life that I can relate to Philip's problem. It is easy to hide behind the term prudent or practical. It is even easier to find a host of people that will tell you that you're doing the right thing by waiting. There were more Israelites that supported the decision to stay on this side of Jordan rather than cross over and possess the land. We need to understand that the majority is not always right.

Philip was a limited Christian. There are several areas that Philip limited himself.

The Pursuit of God *John 1:43-46*
Philip is not the kind of individual that is going to drop everything and run after God. J.D. Jones said, "Philip was a patient inquirer. He has a habit of patient and accurate examination." One old writer called Philip "a slow plodder." Philip is not going to drop the nets like John or turn his back on the seat of customs like Matthew. Rather, Philip is going to continually glean information until he has enough facts to offset his absence of faith.

The entire Christian life is one of faith. *"Therefore being justified by faith, we have peace with God through our Lord Jesus Christ: By whom also we have access by faith into this* grace wherein we stand, and rejoice in hope of the glory of God" (Romans 5:1-2). The foundation of our faith is the truth of God (see Romans 10:17). Faith does not ignore or disregard truth but, acts and responds to the truth. Philip had sufficient truth but was slow in acting upon it.

1. His Request

"And another of his disciples said unto him, Lord, suffer me first to go and bury my father. But Jesus said unto him, Follow me; and let the dead bury their dead" (Matthew 8:21-22). Tradition tells us that this disciple was Philip. It must be understood that Jesus is not encouraging anyone to disregard their responsibility to their family. The Bible teaches us, "But if any provide not for his own, and specially for those of his own house, he hath denied the faith, and is worse than an infidel" (I Timothy 5:8).

It needs to be understood that this disciple's father was not dead. Most likely, the father was doing rather well. What the disciple was saying was, "suffer me first." Are we guilty of saying "me first?" This disciple wanted to go home and continue living life as usual. His thoughts were, one day when my father is dead, when I have received my inheritance, I am financially stable, and I can see how everything is going to take care of itself, then I will come and follow Christ. Listen to Paul's admonishment to the believers at Corinth, "For we walk by faith, not by sight" (II Corinthians 5:7).

How many times do we want to see it or feel it before we drop all and pursue after God? I personally resisted the call to preach for several years because I could not get everything arranged like I thought they needed to be. What blessings and privileges have you missed out on because you could not trust God?

2. His Reservation

"Philip findeth Nathanael . . . Philip saith unto him, Come and see" (John 1:45-46). Did Philip go to Nathanael to share his faith or to establish his faith? It is apparent that Philip and

74

Nathanael shared a common interest in the Word of God and a desire to find the Messiah. They most likely read and studied the Word of God together. They exchanged thoughts on the scriptures and appreciated each other's insight into God's Word. What a blessing to have a friend who delights in conversing about the things of God, an individual with whom you can receive enlightenment on truth. I think, for Philip, Nathanael was the individual he sought out for instruction.

Nathanael can help give light to Philip, but he cannot believe for him. Philip cannot build his faith on Nathanael's faith; he must establish his faith on the truth. There are numerous individuals that have a weak and anemic faith because they are trying to live off of grandma's faith or dad's faith. The basis for your faith should not be, "that is what our family has always believed." I'm sure Nathanael would not have led Philip wrong intentionally. But, what would Philip have done if after Nathanael had met Jesus, Nathanael said, "that's not the Messiah?" Philip must act on the truth of God's Word and not someone else's response to it!

There are people that have reservations about salvation. None of their family or friends have trusted Christ as Saviour, and they're waiting for someone to make the first move. Many wait too long! Many teenagers who have come to know the Lord Jesus Christ as personal Saviour, sit in church just going through the motions, knowing that God wants them to surrender their all to Him. Why the reservation on total commitment? They are waiting on someone else to make the first move.

Philip was hesitant about total commitment to Christ. If he could just get Nathanael to agree that Jesus and the facts lined up, then he would drop everything and pursue hard after God. What are you waiting on?

The Power of God *John 6:5-7*

John 6:5 "When Jesus then lifted up his eyes, and saw a great company come unto him, he saith unto Philip, Whence shall we buy bread, that these may eat?" Philip is confronted with an opportunity to unleash the power of God. Philip begins to quickly jumble all the facts and figures on bread cost, the number present, and bread availability. The answer is, it cannot be done on our budget and our resources. While Philip was calculating and working on the equation, he left out the most important aspect, the potential of God's power. Philip had limited the power of God in his life.

You might be saying to yourself, "I have never limited God's power in my life." Are you sure? James said in his epistle, *"yet ye have not, because ye ask not" (James 4:2).* How many times have I gotten by on meager fare because I failed to just ask God?

Like Philip, each of us must either live and operate in the energy of the flesh or the power of the Spirit. The energy of the flesh cannot answer the challenges of life, God can! What sphere will you choose to live in? God's power is available to us through the Holy Spirit. We need the Spirit for our:

1. Walk
"This I say then, Walk in the Spirit, and ye shall not fulfil the lust of the flesh" (Galatians 5:16). Within the life of every believer is a war that rages. Paul spoke of that war in *Romans 7:21.* The opposing forces are good and evil which are representative of the Spirit and the flesh. If left unchecked, the flesh will gravitate toward sin. The flesh loves sin, lives to sin, and can do nothing but sin. Paul makes this clear in *Galatians 5:16* when he speaks of the *"lust"* of the flesh. The meaning of the word "lust" is a longing, especially for that which is forbidden. Each of us knows what it is to deal with those longings.

If there is no power equal to or greater than that of the flesh, the believer will continue to be pulled into sin. We will *"fulfil"* that lust. To fulfil means to complete, execute, fill up, or perform. The natural man does not have the power nor the desire to stop these longings. Only the Holy Spirit that lives within the believer can crush the power of the flesh. Paul admonishes the child of God to walk at large, follow as a companion, be occupied with the Holy Spirit, and then, the longings of the flesh can be rendered ineffective.

2. Work

"Verily, verily, I say unto you, He that believeth on me, the works that I do shall he do also; and greater works than these shall he do; because I go unto my Father. And whatsoever ye shall ask in my name, that will I do, that the Father may be glorified in the Son" (John 14:12-13). The conflict in the life of the believer continues into our work. Each of us is performing the works of the flesh or the works of God. Jesus told his disciples that they would do even greater works than He did. How is it possible? It would be hard enough to keep from performing the works of the flesh. We would consider ourselves doing good just to execute some works of the Spirit, but that's not what Jesus said. He said, *"greater works!"*

The believer can do greater works because of our High **Priest.** When Jesus went back to the Father, He sat down at the Father's right hand to serve as our High Priest. *"Seeing then that we have a great high priest, that is passed into the heavens, Jesus the Son of God, let us hold fast our profession. For we have not an high priest which cannot be touched with the feeling of our infirmities; but was in all points tempted like as we are, yet without sin. Let us therefore come boldly unto the throne of grace, that we may obtain mercy, and find grace to help in time of need" (Hebrews 4:14-16).* Help is available to us through our High Priest.

The believer can do greater works because of **prayer.** James tells us in his epistle, *"yet ye have not, because ye ask not"*

(James 4:2). God said unto Jeremiah, *"Call unto me, and I will answer thee, and show thee great and mighty things, which thou knowest not" (Jeremiah 33:3).* Prayer is the key that unlocks the resources of heaven, and most of us fail to use it.

The greater works are accomplished through the believer because of a **Paraketos.** *"And I will pray the Father, and he shall give you another Comforter, that he may abide with you for ever; Even the Spirit of truth; whom the world cannot receive, because it seeth him not, neither knoweth him: but ye know him; for he dwelleth with you, and shall be in you" (John 14:16-17).* When Jesus returned to the Father, He not only became our High Priest, but the Holy Spirit (Paraketos), or Comforter, was sent to become our companion and guide. The Holy Spirit would be with us and in us. The believer has power at their disposal because the third person of the Godhead tabernacles within them.

There is no excuse for allowing the works of the flesh to circumvent the works of God in our lives. We have sufficient resources to do the greater works if we will not limit ourselves.

3. Warfare
"For though we walk in the flesh, we do not war after the flesh: (For the weapons of our warfare are not carnal, but mighty through God to the pulling down of strong holds;)" (II Corintians 10:3-4). "For we wrestle not against flesh and blood, but against principalities, against powers, against the rulers of the darkness of this world, against spiritual wickedness in high places" (Ephesians 6:12). Peter tells the children of God about an enemy that walks about seeking to swallow them up. He uses the descriptive term, roaring lion, to describe the fierceness of this adversary *(see 1 Peter 5:8).* If this enemy is to be combated, it has to be done in something other than the energy of the flesh! The warfare that the believer now finds himself in is one that is spiritual. Therefore, the weapons of our warfare must be spiritual weapons. How many of God's children have been casualties of

the war because they failed to use the resources made available to them? Only the power of God is sufficient to overcome Satan and the forces of darkness.

Philip limited the power of God because he did not take advantage of it. Each of us need to avail ourselves of the resource that is ours through Jesus Christ our Lord. We must have the power of God in our walk, work and warfare if we are to bring glory to the Saviour.

The Purpose of God *John 12:21-22*

"And there were certain Greeks among them that came up to worship at the feast: The same came therefore to Philip, which was of Bethsaida of Galilee, and desired him, saying, Sir, we would see Jesus. Philip cometh and telleth Andrew: and again Andrew and Philip tell Jesus" (John 12:20-22). There was a group of Greeks that had come up to the feast to worship. These Greeks were evidently Jewish proselytes that were trying to find God through the means of keeping the law. Whether it was the emptiness of the Jewish rituals, or a curiosity about the words and works of Jesus, the Holy Spirit encouraged these individuals to seek out the Son of God. They came to Philip with a very simple request, *"Sir, we would see Jesus."* Philip had the chance to advance while being part of the purposes of God. What did Philip do with this great opportunity? Philip limited the purposes of God!

God's eternal purposes cannot be overturned by mortal man. God will get these seekers to Jesus. Just as God knew what Philip would do at the feeding of the five thousand, He knew what Philip would do with this opportunity. Philip does not limit God, just as God did not limit Philip. Philip limits himself! This thought would not be too disturbing if Philip did not have to give an account for all these opportunities. *"So then every one of us shall give account of himself to God" (Romans 14:12).* God's Word uses the phrase *"give account"* four times. Studying these references reveals an accountability for our walk, words, and works. In light of the judgment, things are getting a little more serious.

God's purposes in Philip's life were limited in several areas. One of God's purposes for Philip was to **shine.** *"Neither do men light a candle, and put it under a bushel, but on a candlestick; and it giveth light unto all that are in the house. Let your light so shine before men, that they may see your good works, and glorify your Father which is in heaven" (Matthew 5:15-16).* Philip had the opportunity to let his light shine before these Greeks, and he hid it. Was it because of fear? I do not know the why, but I know that the light of the glorious gospel was hid by Philip. I personally cannot be too quick to judge Philip, for I find myself failing to give forth the light as I should.

When Philip did not bring the Greeks to Jesus, he limited his **service** to God. Philip not only failed to shine before the Greeks, but he failed to serve his Lord and Saviour, Jesus Christ. Philip was to serve the Lord by taking Christ to all men. Each of us have been given the same command *(see II Corinthians 5:18-21)*. Philip had not only failed in the operation of service, but he had failed in the opportunity of service. Jesus had reached out to every other outcast group, the Gentiles, the Samaritans, Publicans, and sinners; why would Philip think Jesus would exclude these Greeks? The only qualification for being a recipient of the gospel is that an individual be a sinner. All men fall into that class. *"For all have sinned, and come short of the glory of God" (Romans 3:23).*

Philip will give an account for the opportunities given him to be part of God's eternal purposes. Philip's response to those opportunities will determine his rewards. Just as Philip must stand before the Lord, you and I must do the same. May we determine not to limit God's purposes in our lives!

The Person of God *John 14:8-9*

John 14:9 "Jesus saith unto him, Have I been so long time with you, and yet hast thou not known me, Philip? he that hath seen me hath seen the Father; and how sayest thou then, Show us the Father?" For over three years, Philip has traversed the countryside with Jesus. He has listened to Christ's words, seen His works, but failed to grasp the fact that Jesus is God in the flesh. Philip has opened his head to facts but not his heart to feeling. This is not only the story of Philip, but this is the story of most of God's children. It is one thing to know about God; it is quite another to know God.

Listen to the words of our Lord, *"Have I been so long time with you."* The word used for "long" means so vast as this. Jesus is saying to Philip, "we have been together for a long time!" Yet, with such a great opportunity afforded Philip, he has not made use of it. Philip has not taken the time to get to know the Lord Jesus. The word "know" means to be aware, have knowledge of, understand, or to be sure. Philip is still living life with a big question mark at the end. Is this the description of your personal relationship with God?

Just because someone has been saved for twenty years or longer does not mean that they have an intimate relationship with the Lord. Many are not sure that God loves them. They still think love is tied to prosperity. Some remain weak in faith. They are not sure of the promises of God.

Philip was trying to live life according to the natural eye rather than the eye of faith. How much do you know about the person of God? Do you have an intimate personal relationship with God? The only way this is possible is to pursue after God and the things of God. *"Draw nigh to God, and he will draw nigh to you" (James 4:8).* You are only as close to God as you want to be. David knew God because he longed after Him! *"As the hart panteth after the water brooks, so panteth my soul after thee, O God" (Psalms 42:1).* Intimacy with and information about God is not due to longevity but longing and love. One old writer said, "The hardest thing I have to do is get my people to love a God they do not know."

If Philip had not limited himself in the pursuit of God, the power of God, and the purposes of God, he would have known God because it is the natural outgrowth of them. Knowledge would have come from pursuit. Assurance would have been generated from the demonstration of His power. And, peace would have come from fulfilling God's purposes.

Philip hid behind the terms levelheaded, practical, and prudent. What are you hiding behind? He had all the right opportunities, but he never took advantage of them. Will you take advantage of the opportunities, or will you be a limited Christian?

Chapter Seven

Nathanael, the Devoted Christian

John 1:45-51 "Philip findeth Nathanael, and saith unto him, We have found him, of whom Moses in the law, and the prophets, did write, Jesus of Nazareth, the son of Joseph. And Nathanael said unto him, Can there any good thing come out of Nazareth? Philip saith unto him, Come and see. Jesus saw Nathanael coming to him, and saith of him, Behold an Israelite indeed, in whom is no guile! Nathanael saith unto him, Whence knowest thou me? Jesus answered and said unto him, Before that Philip called thee, when thou wast under the fig tree, I saw thee. Nathanael answered and saith unto him, Rabbi, thou art the Son of God; thou art the King of Israel. Jesus answered and said unto him, Because I said unto thee, I saw thee under the fig tree, believest thou? thou shalt see greater things than these. And he saith unto him, Verily, verily, I say unto you, Hereafter ye shall see heaven open, and the angels of God ascending and descending upon the Son of man.

Nathanael and Philip were close friends. Their friendship was apparently built around the search for the Messiah. It was Philip that brought Nathanael word that they had found him of whom Moses and the prophets did write. Nathanael was from Cana of Galilee which was about eleven miles from Nazareth. In Luke's gospel, Nathanael is referred to by the name Bartholomew.

There appears to be nothing extraordinary about Nathanael, and most would place him in the common lump of humanity. But, upon close inspection, there is one spiritual characteristic that pushes Nathanael to the front of the pack. Nathanael was a man of devotion. Every aspect of his life appears to be devoted to

God. Nathanael's life is marked by dedication, consecration, loyalty, and faithfulness. This is what it means to be devoted! Are these characteristics prevalent in your relationship to the Lord Jesus Christ?

J.Golder Burns said of Nathanael, "He was not the type whose religion is simply that of tradition and authority, in which case it remains merely one of the chance and occasional interest of life." As I read this, my heart was grieved to think of the absence of devotion among the Christian community. Most would have to describe their relationship to God as an "occasional interest in life." This was not the case in Nathanael's life!

There are several areas of devotion in Nathanael's life that we would do well to emulate in our own. Nathanael was devoted to:

A Place

"Before that Philip called thee, when thou wast under the fig tree, I saw thee" (John 1:48). After being introduced to the Lamb of God by John the Baptist, Philip sought out Nathanael. Did Philip just wander around and by chance happen to stumble on Nathanael? No! Because they were friends, Philip knew the habits of his friend. He knew exactly where Nathanael would be at this particular time. Nathanael would be in his private place of worship under the fig tree.

The fig tree was like a private room. Because of the poverty in Palestine, the construction of most homes was small and humble. There was not a lot of privacy, so they would plant a fig tree in the garden attached to the house. The fig tree would reach about fifteen feet in height, but its limbs would spread out as much as twenty-five feet. If an individual wanted to be alone, they would go out under the fig tree.

Nathanael was devoted to a place where he could meet with God. Knowing the time of day, Philip knew exactly where his friend would be. I wonder if you have developed any habits like

Nathanael. Do your friends, neighbors, family, and associates know that you are devoted to a place? There are two places each of us needs to be devoted to.

1. Our Closet

"But thou, when thou prayest, enter into thy closet, and when thou hast shut thy door, pray to thy Father which is in secret; and thy Father which seeth in secret shall reward thee openly" (Matthew 6:6). When Nathanael went out under the fig tree, it was a time to be alone with God. It was a private time. It was to be a time of intimacy. What happened during that closet time determined what happened in the public times. Could it be the reason nothing is going on in public is because nothing is going on in private?

I have just finished reading "Victorious Christians You Should Know" by Warren Wiersbe. The book consists of short biographical sketches of great Christians. While these individuals live in different times and places, there were several things they had in common. One area of common ground was a devotional time with their Heavenly Father. Have you established a practice of meeting with the Lord? A time when you close out the world and enter into a time of choice intimacy. The songwriter G.T. Byrd said it best when he wrote, "There are days to fast and pray for the pilgrim in his way, There are days to be with Christ all alone, We can tell him all our grief, He will give us quick relief, There are days I'd like to be just all alone."

This was not only a practice of great Christians, it was the practice of Christ! *"And in the morning, rising up a great while before day, he went out, and departed into a solitary place, and there prayed" (Mark 1:35).* Christ was totally dependent upon His Father for everything. Because of this, it was imperative that He spend time with the Father. We need not be reminded that we too are totally dependent creatures!

2. Our Church

"Not forsaking the assembling of ourselves together, as the manner of some is; but exhorting one another: and so much the more, as ye see the day approaching" (Hebrews 10:25). Because of Nathanael's diligent study of God's Word, he knew the importance of being present at all the annual feasts. Nathanael would be devoted to the House of Worship!

We are living in a day when professing Christians are anything but devoted to the House of God. Most join the church with no intention of supporting it with their time, talents, and monetary means. The same individual that would never think of missing a meeting of the bass club, doll club, or some civic club looks for any excuse to avoid going to church. Some would say that one can make a god of church. While that may be so, most that are worried about that sin have made a god of something else.

Philip knew where his friend would be because Nathanael was devoted to a place. He was devoted to a place of intimacy and worship. What kind of place are you devoted to?

A Practice
"Thou shalt see greater things than these. And he saith unto him, Verily, verily, I say unto you, Hereafter ye shall see heaven open, and the angels of God ascending and descending upon the Son of man" (John 1:50-51). What was Nathanael doing out under the fig tree? Was the fig tree just a place to get out of the house or away from the family? No! It was a place that Nathanael carried out religious practices. Nathanael was devoted to the practice of meeting with God under the fig tree daily. From the conversation between Jesus and Nathanael, it becomes apparent that Nathanael was devoted to at least two practices.

1. Meditation on the Word
Nathanael practiced meditating upon the Word of God. From what Philip said to Nathanael when he told him of finding the Messiah, *"We have found him, of whom Moses in the law, and the prophets, did write" (John 1:45),* it is apparent that

Nathanael is a student of the Word of God. If Nathanael was to recognize the Messiah and not be deceived as most of Israel was, he must have a good grasp on Bible truth.

Nathanael's devotion to the Word of God is illustrated by Jesus' conversation with Nathanael. Most feel that *verses 50-51* have reference to what Nathanael was studying when Philip found him under the fig tree. Jesus speaks of angels ascending and descending upon the Son of God. Because of this reference, many feel Nathanael was studying and reading in *Genesis 28:12, "And he dreamed, and behold a ladder set up on the earth, and the top of it reached to heaven: and behold the angels of God ascending and descending on it."*

If we are to keep from being deceived by the false teachers of today's religious cults, we will have to be devoted to the practice of meditating on the Word of God. Paul instructed Timothy with these words, *"Study to show thyself approved unto God, a workman that needeth not to be ashamed, rightly dividing the word of truth" (II Timothy 2:15).* Why is the church the greatest mission field for the cults? The answer is our ignorance of the Word of God. They pitch out a damnable lie cloaked with some Bible verse, and the ignorant gobble it up.

The blessed man in *Psalm 1* is firmly planted, flourishing, and fruitful. What is the reason for such a blessed life? Could it be, *"But his delight is in the law of the LORD; and in his law doth he meditate day and night" (Psalms 1:2)?* I think so! Is your mind preoccupied with the Word of God or the things of the world?

2. Meditation in Prayer
Nathanael was a man of the book and a man of prayer. Nathanael knew that God had the answer to all his needs. William Law, in "Serious Call," said "Pray always in the same place; reserve that place of devotion, and never allow yourself to do anything common in it." The Bible reveals that Isaac had a

green field *(Genesis 24:63),* Elijah had a mountain cave *(I Kings 19:9),* Jesus had a garden *(John 18:1),* and Nathanael had a fig tree.

We are admonished by the Word, *"Pray without ceasing. In every thing give thanks" (I Thessalonians 5:17-18).* By word *(see Luke 18)*, and example, Jesus encouraged his followers to pray.

Great Christians put a premium on prayer and Bible study. We must emulate Nathanael's devotion to the practice of meditation on the Word and meditation in prayer!

A Purity

"Jesus saw Nathanael coming to him, and saith of him, Behold an Israelite indeed, in whom is no guile" (John 1:47)! These are not the words of Nathanael in regard to how he feels about himself, rather, they are the words of our Lord. The words of one that knows everything. Nathanael desired to be pure before the Lord. Jesus reveals two areas of Nathanael's purity.

1. Pure Motives

"In whom is no guile" (John 1:47)! When Jesus refers to Nathanael as an individual *"in whom is no guile,"* he is projecting the idea of a "straight man." This is the opposite of that trickster Jacob. Jacob had anything but pure motives when he dealt with his father, brother, uncle, wife, and even God. We have forgotten that in order to be the right kind of person, one must not only act right, but one must also think right! Nathanael did not approach Jesus with a "what's in it for me" attitude.

2. Pure Methods

"Behold an Israelite indeed, in whom is no guile" (John 1:47)! When one's motives are right, one's methods will be right. Newman said, "The guileless man found in *Psalm 15:2, "He that walketh uprightly, and worketh righteousness, and speaketh the truth in his heart."* Jesus also refers to Nathanael as *"an*

Israelite indeed." There were two kinds of seed in Israel, physical seed and seed of promise. The physical seed were those that simply claimed to be part of Israel because they were Abraham's descendants. Nathanael was more than a descendant of Abraham, he was one who walked by faith, looking for the coming Messiah. Nathanael was an individual that strove to align his walk with the Word.

We are commanded by God to be pure! *"But as he which hath called you is holy, so be ye holy in all manner of conversation; Because it is written, Be ye holy; for I am holy" (I Peter 1:15-16). "Wherefore come out from among them, and be ye separate, saith the Lord, and touch not the unclean thing; and I will receive you" (II Corinthians 6:17).* A devotion to being pure is a sure way to please your Heavenly Father.

A Person

"Nathanael answered and saith unto him, Rabbi, thou art the Son of God; thou art the King of Israel" (John 1:49). Nathanael's devotion to the person of Christ can be seen in two ways.

1. His Witness
When Nathanael responded to Christ, he used three titles. In each of these areas, Nathanael was devoted to his Lord.
(a) *Rabbi*
When Nathanael used this title, we knew he was devoted to the **Lordship of Christ.** The word Rabbi means my master, an official title of honor. There are four times Jesus is called Rabbi; *John 1:38* by John, *John 1:49* by Nathanael, *John 3:2* by Nicodemus, and *John 6:25* by the multitude. In each reference, we can see an area of Christ Lordship. Christ is master of salvation, sovereignty, scriptures, and supply. Jesus Christ is Lord of all. In the next three years, Nathanael would know Christ in all four of these areas.
(b) *Son of God*
This title speaks of the **Deity of Christ.** Nathanael declared that

Jesus was not just from God but that He was God.

(c) *King of Israel*

This title tells us that Christ is the **Sovereign Ruler** or **King of Kings**. Nathanael had been looking for the one that would sit upon the throne of his father, David; and the promised Messiah had come, and His name was Jesus.

Do you have an experiential knowledge that Jesus is Lord, God, and King? Experiential knowledge is not a head knowledge but a heart knowledge. The heart knowledge is the one of value!

2. His Waiting

"And when they were come in, they went up into an upper room, where abode both Peter, and James, and John, and Andrew, Philip, and Thomas, Bartholomew, and Matthew, James the son of Alphaeus, and Simon Zelotes, and Judas the brother of James" (Acts 1:13). After over three years, Nathanael, also known as Bartholomew, was still devoted to the person of Christ. He has withstood the difficult times of adversity, the criticism of the Pharisees, the persecution of the religious leaders, and the trial of the cross. Jesus has now returned to the side of the Father on high, and where do we find this devoted Christian? Nathanael is waiting in the upper room just like his Sovereign said.

Are we devoted to the person of Christ? Do we yield to His Lordship, to His Deity, and to Him as King? Or, do we rejoice in His salvation and reject His Sovereign rule over our lives? If one is to be devoted to the person of Christ, it will be manifested in our witness and our waiting.

Each of us may find ourselves in the same position as Nathanael, no extraordinary talents or abilities. While we may be common in our physical makeup, we can be superior in spiritual devotion. Nathanael was uncommon in his devotion to **a Place**, **a Practice**, **Purity**, and **a Person**. To whom and what are you devoted?

Chapter Eight

Matthew, the Open Christian

Matthew 9:9 "And as Jesus passed forth from thence, he saw a man, named Matthew, sitting at the receipt of custom: and he saith unto him, Follow me. And he arose, and followed him."

When Jesus found Matthew, he was seated at the receipt of customs, collecting taxes for the government of Rome. Matthew was a Jew that sold out to the enemy. Pleasure meant more to him than patriotism. Sometimes Matthew was referred to as Levi in the Scriptures.

When reading and studying the life of Matthew, there is one thing that jumps out about this man. It is his openness. Matthew is not an individual with dual personalities. Some would say, "what you see is what you get," or "I can read him like a book." Matthew may be a publican, but he is no Pharisee!

I love people like Matthew. Right or wrong, Matthew is sold out and everybody knows it! How repulsive to be around someone that acts one way with this crowd and another way with the other crowd. It makes one wonder what they say about you when you're not around. I want to be transparent like Matthew. Wherever I am, I want to be the same individual. When I first started into evangelism, an old preacher said to me, "Just be what you are. Do not try to be something you're not just to please a group of people. The day will come when you forget how you acted with them, and they will see you for what you really are. So, just be what you are!"

There are four areas in which it is apparent that Matthew does not mind you seeing all. Matthew was open when it came to:

His Mistakes

Listen to the way Matthew describes himself when giving a list of the twelve, *"Matthew the publican" (Matthew 10:3)*. Matthew is the only one of the apostles that refers to himself as being a publican. The only other reference is in Doctor Luke's account of Matthew's conversion. Here, the reference is informative and not given to belittle.

While others would cover Matthew's mistakes, as well as their own, not Matthew. Matthew has no problem telling others about his mistakes. This may have been one of the many things Jesus appreciated about this man. Our Lord cared nothing for a pharisaic spirit. Listen to these words by the Lord Jesus, *"Woe unto you, scribes and Pharisees, hypocrites! for ye are like unto whited sepulchers, which indeed appear beautiful outward, but are within full of dead men's bones, and of all uncleanness. Even so ye also outwardly appear righteous unto men, but within ye are full of hypocrisy and iniquity" (Matthew 23:27-28).* Our Lord cared nothing for the pharisaical spirit when He walked on this earth, and He has not changed His mind.

Most of us fail to understand the class of people Matthew had aligned himself with. Only a full knowledge of what it meant to be a publican will make you appreciate the openness of this man.

1. Their Walk

When it came to publicans, the religious crowd generally lumped them together with a class called sinners. An example of this is *Luke 5:30* when the scribes and Pharisees murmured against the Lord's disciples, saying, *"Why do ye eat and drink with publicans and sinners?"* The publicans and sinners were perceived as a vile bunch, not fit for the blessings of God but rather fit subjects for hell.

I do not know what was considered lower, but it was said that there was only one degree of shame lower than publicans and sinners. This was the reason the Pharisee in *Luke 18:11* said, *"God, I thank thee, that I am not as other men are, extortioners, unjust, adulterers, or even as this publican."*

Matthew was open when it came to his walk. He did not try to hide it but openly admitted that this was the lifestyle he lived prior to being saved. While our past is nothing to brag about, each of us should readily admit where God found us and out of what He brought us.

2. Their Word

Matthew had not only had problems with his life but with his lips as well. If one were to ask the common people of Matthew's day, they would tell you that they regarded it impossible for a publican to tell the truth. A publican's word was so bad that their testimony was refused in the courts of their day. Publicans were considered incapable of taking an oath.

Can you remember what your speech was like before God saved you? Listen to God's description of the sinner's word, *"Their throat is an open sepulchre; with their tongues they have used deceit; the poison of asps is under their lips: Whose mouth is full of cursing and bitterness" (Romans 3:13-14).*

3. Their Wealth

The manner in which publicans acquired their money was anything but honest. Most publicans came into their wealth by means of a corrupt walk and corrupt words. A publican's money was so tainted that it would not be accepted in the synagogue.

4. Their Work

Matthew did not have a praiseworthy job. As a matter of fact, being a publican was a despised occupation. If a Jew chose to be a publican, they abandoned all sense of patriotism. There were very few occupations that were looked down upon with the same degree of resentment as that of a publican.

While many will try to cover their past, Matthew was an open book. Matthew was not proud of his previous walk, word, wealth, or work, but he did not try to whitewash his past with religious deeds. Rather, Matthew openly revealed that this was the kind of life out of which God had brought him. Are you open about your mistakes?

His Money

No other writer speaks more openly about money and its effects on the souls of men. I am well aware of the fact that nothing will kill a meeting any quicker than a preacher talking about money. Why is that? Could it be because money occupies the wrong place in most of our lives?

Matthew was not giving us secondhand information about money; this was the voice of experience. J. Golder Burns said, "As no other Disciple, Matthew could preach the dangers of riches." Please note four things Matthew had to say about money:

1. The Loyalty of Money

"For where your treasure is, there will your heart be also" (Matthew 6:21).

Webster describes treasure as anything that a person considers valuable. Matthew was telling us that whatever a man places the most value on, that will be the thing he loves the most. If an individual's treasure is money, then that person's heart will convince them to give themselves totally to acquiring and hoarding up money.

All of us will remain loyal to whatever occupies the throne of our heart! At one time, the throne of Matthew's heart was occupied by money, thus making him loyal to it. On what do you place the greatest value? Whatever it is, your heart will demand loyalty to it.

2. The Loss of Money

"Lay not up for yourselves treasures upon earth, where moth and rust doth corrupt, and where thieves break through and steal: But lay up for yourselves treasures in heaven, where neither moth nor rust doth corrupt, and where thieves do not break through nor steal" (Matthew 6:19-20)

Matthew points out that there is a loss of everyone's money. He was not speaking of a stock market crash or high inflation. Matthew was speaking of the temporal versus the eternal. While money may have some value in this temporal sphere, it is worthless in the world to come.

Each of us can give ourselves to acquiring houses, lands, and the wealth of the world, but when a person crosses from time into eternity, the next world will not acknowledge the temporal worth of earth's riches.

Matthew realized that the currency of heaven was not in garments, grain, or gold. May I remind you neither is it the British pound, the Japanese yen, or the U.S. dollars.

3. The Lordship of Money

"No man can serve two masters: for either he will hate the one, and love the other; or else he will hold to the one, and despise the other. Ye cannot serve God and mammon" (Matthew 6:24).

Matthew points out several things about lordship in the life of an individual. There is but one throne in the heart of man. While there may be several valuable and worthwhile things competing for the throne, only one master can occupy that throne. Whatever, or whoever, occupies that throne is lord of that individual's life.

The lordship question is settled by the simple test of love. That which you love the most is given the throne. While it may be embarrassing and we will not admit it even to ourselves, Christ has been dethroned by the material wealth of the world. Curtis Hutson said, "On our money we have written, In God we trust, when probably for many it would be more correct to say, In this god we trust."

4. The Littleness of Money

"For what is a man profited, if he shall gain the whole world, and lose his own soul? or what shall a man give in exchange for his soul" (Matthew 16:26)?

When listening to the news about the nation's or the world's economy, they will give statistics concerning inflation. This is a term that speaks about the buying power of money in reference to the past. All of us have heard it said, "You can't buy what you use to for a dollar."

While the value of money is diminishing all the time, to understand the true worth, Matthew tells us to compare the temporal to the eternal. When this is done, the littleness of money can be seen. If a man could gain everything that his heart desired and did not know the Lord Jesus Christ as personal Saviour, that person would not have enough material wealth to purchase his own soul from the eternal abode of the damned.

When speaking of the effect of money on a person, Matthew is speaking from personal experience. Money had lorded over Matthew's life but no more. William McIntyre said, when speaking of Matthew's response to follow Christ, "He probably gave up more than any other disciple to follow Christ." I do not know how much of this world's riches you may possess, but if you have never accepted Christ as your personal Saviour, leave all and go to Him.

His Master

And after these things he went forth, and saw a publican, named Levi, sitting at the receipt of custom: and he said unto him, Follow me. And he left all, rose up, and followed him. And Levi made him a great feast in his own house: and there was a great company of publicans and of others that sat down with them" (Luke 5:27-29).

96

Matthew had been dominated and ruled over by money. Matthew openly served and yielded to the wishes and desires of that master until a new master came along. One day, while seated at the receipt of custom, Jesus Christ passed by. Walking past, Jesus said unto Matthew, *"Follow me."* Matthew left the old master of money to follow his new master, the Lord Jesus Christ.

Matthew had not been bashful about his loyalty and love for the old master, and he was not going to be any different about the new master. The first thing Matthew did to reveal his love and loyalty to Christ was prepare a great feast in honor of his new master. He then invited all to come and meet this new master.

Matthew's feast revealed several things about the way he felt about his new master. Matthew was not ashamed about these feelings and wanted all to know.

1. The Worth of His Master

In *verse 28,* when Matthew rose from the seat of custom and left all, Matthew was saying, **"Christ is worth leaving all."** Matthew was from Capernaum, and in those days, it was a sort of cross-roads of the world. Armies, caravans, and individuals laden with goods passed by Matthew's office. Matthew gave up prestige, power, and position to follow one who had no place to lay His head. There was nothing that was worth holding onto at the expense of losing Christ.

What is it that you will not relinquish from your grasp? Listen to this powerful statement by Gaston Foote, "Jesus' chief condemnation was never against a man's past but against his unwillingness to respond to the future."

In *verse 29,* when Matthew prepared the great feast, Matthew is saying, **"Christ is worth giving all."** Matthew did not stop at leaving the seat of custom, but what he possessed he poured out to lavish his love upon the Saviour. Matthew would not withhold anything from Christ. If he thought it would please, honor, or magnify the Saviour, Matthew gladly placed it upon the altar of love.

While you have come to Christ for salvation, are there areas of your life that you have put up no trespassing signs? Are there small strongholds of lust, pleasure, or sin you are unwilling to give to Him?

Matthew was not ashamed of his new master! Whether it be in the past or the future, Matthew's hands were open to the Saviour.

2. The Witness for His Master

The large feast that Matthew gave in honor of the Lord Jesus not only spoke of His worth but also served as a witness for Christ. Matthew's witness was **public**. When Matthew accepted the call to follow the Lord, he did not take Jesus to his home under the cover of darkness. Matthew had been public about his sin, and he would now be public about the Saviour. Note in *verse 29* it speaks of a *"great feast,"* and a *"great company."* Matthew was not going to be a secret disciple, as if there is such a thing. Are you bold in your public witness for Christ? Listen to the words of our Lord, *"Whosoever therefore shall be ashamed of me and of my words in this adulterous and sinful generation; of him also shall the Son of man be ashamed, when he cometh in the glory of his Father with the holy angels" (Mark 8:38).*

Matthew had a **powerful** witness. His openness not only caught the eye of the religious crowd but their scorn as well, *"But their scribes and Pharisees murmured" (Luke 5:30).* It was evident to all that there had been a change in the life of Matthew. *"Therefore if any man be in Christ, he is a new creature: old things are passed away; behold, all things are become new" (II Corinthians 5:17).* It was obvious to all that Christ had made a new man out of this detestable individual. Religion had not been able to do it! Social reform had not been able to do it! This new creature was a testimony of what only Christ can do in a life.

The feast revealed a **personal** witness. When the guest list was made up for the great feast, Matthew did not invite individuals that had no knowledge of his past. The guests were not strangers but rather old friends with whom he had wallowed in sin, *"and there was a great company of publicans and of others that sat down with them" (Luke 5:29).* Matthew wanted his old friends to see the new man. While Matthew may have been ashamed of his past, he was not ashamed of what Christ had done.

The openness of Matthew about his new master puts some of us to shame. Do I have the same fervent love for the Lord that Matthew had? A good way to test our love is to investigate and see how open we are when it comes to Christ.

His Message

Matthew was a man with a message. Matthew's voice would not be silenced by time or tribulation. He would speak freely and openly with life and lips.

1. His Penned Epistle

Alexander Whyte said, "When Matthew rose up and left all and followed our Lord, the only thing he took with him out of his old occupation was his pen and ink." After the Old Testament canon of scripture had been closed for hundreds of years, God began to speak again with what we know as the New Testament. The church fathers, guided by the Holy Spirit, placed the message of Matthew at the beginning of the new canon. Gaston Foote said, "When Christ touches the heart, the instruments of evil become instruments for good."

Matthew's message begins with the prophetic birth of Christ and closes with the powerful resurrection of Christ. In Matthew's gospel, Jesus is projected as the King of Kings. While Matthew followed the course of all men, he died, but his message still continues to comfort and gladden the souls of men.

2. His Personal Epistle

Matthew disappears from history after the record of the great feast, but tradition says that he went on to evangelize Ethiopia and Persia. Matthew knew the value of a personal life as well as a penned letter. Paul said, *"Ye are our epistle written in our hearts, known and read of all men: Forasmuch as ye are manifestly declared to be the epistle of Christ ministered by us, written not with ink, but with the Spirit of the living God; not in tables of stone, but in fleshly tables of the heart" (II Corinthians 3:2-3).* Someone once said, "If you talk the talk, walk the walk!" In the epistle to the believers at Philippi, Paul said, *"That ye may be blameless and harmless, the sons of God, without rebuke, in the midst of a crooked and perverse nation, among whom ye shine as lights in the world; Holding forth the word of life; that I may rejoice in the day of Christ, that I have not run in vain, neither laboured in vain" (Philippians 2:15-16).* May each of us strive to have a way of life that matches the words from our lips. While Matthew was a publican, he was no Pharisee.

Matthew was a man that had nothing to hide. One thing that was projected from his life was an openness about his mistakes, his money, his master, and his message. He was just an individual, happy being himself. In these days of deception, it is refreshing to find a transparent individual. What you see is what you get! We would do well to follow the pattern of this humble servant.

Chapter Nine

Thomas, the Doubting Christian

Matthew 10:2-3 "Now the names of the twelve apostles are these; The first, Simon, who is called Peter, and Andrew his brother; James the son of Zebedee, and John his brother; Philip, and Bartholomew; Thomas."

Thomas was born in Antioch and was closely associated with Matthew and Philip. Thomas is also referred to as Didymus in the Scriptures. William McIntyre said, "The real name of Thomas, according to historians, is Judas, or Didymus, meaning a twin. Tradition says he had a twin sister, Lydia, or that he was the twin to another disciple." Thomas is hardly mentioned in the first three gospels, and most of the information about him comes to us from John's writings.

In my search for the central theme of Thomas' life, it was my purpose to stay away from the word "doubt." I do not know if I just wanted to be original or wanted to rebel against the traditional view of "doubting Thomas." Whatever my reasons were, I found that I had to give way to the facts! The facts all point to the one central truth about this man known as Thomas, he was filled with doubt! The dictionary gives this definition for doubt, to be uncertain, mistrust, consider unlikely, inclination not to believe. If they were to have put a picture beside the word "doubt," Thomas' picture would have been the one they would have chosen.

One writer said, "Doubters are always disturbing elements in an atmosphere of faith." Each of us would like to think ourselves as great men and women of faith. Yet, most of us have felt or know what it is to live with the tremors of doubt that shake and destroy peace in our lives. When we find ourselves in the grip of doubt, we can either deny that it exists, excuse it as reasonable, or deal with it.

In *Mark 9*, Jesus came down from the Mount of Transfiguration and sees a great crowd of people gathered about the disciples. A father has brought his son to them to be healed of a dumb spirit *(verse 17)*. Jesus immediately confronts the disciples with their faithlessness and turns to the father. Jesus says to the man, *"If thou canst believe, all things are possible to him that believeth" (verse 23)*. Please note how this man deals with his doubts and fears. *"And straightway the father of the child cried out, and said with tears, Lord, I believe; help thou mine unbelief" (verse 24)*. If we are to dispel the doubt from our lives, we must admit that it is there and turn to the Lord for strength.

The Scriptures reveal three areas in Thomas' life that doubt was prevalent *(John 11:7-16, John 14: 1-7, & John 20: 19-31)*. Each of us can maintain the spirit of a Pharisee and carefully scrutinize these weak areas in Thomas' life while ignoring deficient areas in our lives. Or, we can contrast the weakness of Thomas to areas of need in our own personal life. If areas of need are detected, let us cry in unison with this distraught father, *"help thou mine unbelief!"* Look with me at Thomas, the doubting Christian.

Doubt's Response

The gospel of John records for us three different times where Thomas could have responded in faith to difficult situations. Faith is a positive response which yields itself to peace in the life of the believer. Doubt is a negative response, and it yields fear. Doubt and fear are inseparable. Doubt gives way to fear, and fear encourages doubt. They are like Siamese twins that cannot be separated because they share a major organ. In this case, it is the heart. Because of doubt, there was more fear in the heart of Thomas than faith. Fear and faith cannot coexist in the same

102

heart at the same time. An example of this is in *Matthew 8:23-27,* where Jesus and the disciples were caught in a storm in the midst of the sea. While the Lord was sleeping, a terrible storm had engulfed the small ship so that the scriptures say, *"there arose a great tempest in the sea, insomuch that the ship was covered with the waves" (verse 24).* The disciples cry out unto the Lord to save them. Listen to the response of the Lord Jesus, *"Why are ye fearful, O ye of little faith" (verse 26)?* One cannot be fearful and full of faith at the same time! The fear of the sea had driven faith from the hearts of the disciples. The Greek word translated "fearful" means, dread or timid by implying faithless.

In studying each one of the three situations where Thomas responded in doubt rather than faith, three prevalent fears manifested themselves. Looking at each one of these fears, I quickly arrived at the opinion that they are the same three fears that concern most of us.

1. Fear of the Foe

In *John 11,* word has come to Jesus that a close personal friend by the name of Lazarus is sick. In this troubling moment, Lazarus' sisters had sent for the master to come and heal their brother. Two days after hearing of his friend's condition, Jesus said to His disciples, *"Let us go into Judaea again" (verse 7).* Thomas did not doubt that Jesus could heal Lazarus or even raise him from the dead. Thomas had personal knowledge that Jesus had already healed the nobleman's son, fed five thousand with five loaves and a few fishes, walked on the water, and gave a blind man his sight. When Thomas received word Jesus was going back to Judaea, his response was, *"Let us also go, that we may die with him" (verse 16).* The doubt of Thomas was fueled by fear of the **foe.** This is made clear by *verse 8. "His disciples say unto him, Master, the Jews of late sought to stone thee; and goest thou thither again?"* Thomas as well as the rest of the disciples, were fearful of the Jews and did not want to return to Judaea.

The Bible exposes this fear in *Proverbs 29:25, "The fear of man bringeth a snare: but whoso putteth his trust in the LORD shall be safe."* Many of us find our lives complicated because of this fear. In recent days, the fear of man has been given a new name. We call it peer pressure. Regardless of what you call it, doubt is manifested by this fear! How many of God's children are living substandard lives because they are afraid someone will be critical of them if they sell out totally to God? The young person that would carry their Bible to school if the other kids did not laugh at them. The man that will not pray over his lunch at the factory because the other men see Christianity as something for weaklings. The lady that wears questionable attire because the girls kid her about dressing like an "old lady." The man of God that avoids certain subjects on sin in his sermons because they are not socially acceptable and will effect his popularity among the congregation.

This fear of man brings with it a snare. The word "snare" is a very graphic term. It has reference to a noose for catching animals or a hook for the nose. The fear of man will put a hook in your nose and will lead you about. It will cause you to go places and to do things you normally would not do. In opposition to the fear of man is trust in the Lord. One shall be safe when they trust in the Lord. The word "safe" means to be made inaccessible by implying set upon high. Every one of us are either free in faith, or we are snared in doubt. One is the life of peace while the other is the life of fear!

When speaking to His followers, He said, *"What I tell you in darkness, that speak ye in light: and what ye hear in the ear, that preach ye upon the housetops. And fear not them which kill the body, but are not able to kill the soul: but rather fear him which is able to destroy both soul and body in hell" (Matthew 10:27-28).* Whom do you fear? God or man? The fear of the Lord is the beginning of wisdom *(see Psalms 111:10 & Proverbs 9:10)*, and the fear of man is a snare.

2. Fear of the Future

Jesus, for some time, had been trying to prepare His disciples for His exodus. The Lord's future contained a cross previous to a crown. He would liberate the total man by means of death rather than the physical man by means of insurrection. The disciples had previously had their future worked out. The Christ would come and crush the iron rule of Rome. He would take the throne of David and cause the nation of Israel to become the greatest nation on planet earth. There would be none that could stand against them and His faithful followers would rule with Him. It was then that Jesus began to talk about going away. *"And if I go and prepare a place for you, I will come again, and receive you unto myself; that where I am, there ye may be also. And whither I go ye know, and the way ye know"* (John 14:3-4). When Thomas hears these words, fear of the **future** rose in his heart, and he replies, *"Lord, we know not whither thou goest; and how can we know the way" (John 14:5)?*

Thomas' answer reveals three areas of concern about the future. When he said, *"we know not,"* it speaks of the **darkness of the future**. The word "know" is a verb used only in certain past tenses. It has the idea of what one has seen, known, or been aware of. It speaks totally of the past and not what is yet to be revealed. It is because Thomas did not know what would take place in the future that fear gripped his heart. He rejoiced in the light of yesterday while cringing with fear when he thought of the darkness of tomorrow. If he just knew everything that awaited him in the future, things would have been all right, or so he thought. Jesus said, *"Take therefore no thought for the morrow: for the morrow shall take thought for the things of itself. Sufficient unto the day is the evil thereof" (Matthew 6:34).* The songwriter was scriptural when he said, "I don't know about tomorrow . . . but I know who holds tomorrow." Jesus will be there to see each of us through.

Thomas was fearful of the **destination of the future**. He said, *"whither thou goest."* The word "whither" has the thought of questioning a place or locality. The word "goest" means to withdraw as if sinking out of sight. Thomas' thoughts were that Jesus was going to withdraw from his sight to a place of which he had no knowledge of its location. With Jesus gone, Thomas has no idea where the future is going to take him. Is this not the fear of many of us? We are unsure of where life is going to take us and are not sure we will like it when we get there. Each of us has our own ideas of what is required to make one happy. We fear God may take us somewhere we do not want to go and put us in a place we cannot be happy. Our problem is we want to assert our will over God's will. What we have failed to realize is that we have limited knowledge, and He has all knowledge.

Thomas had doubts about the **direction of the future**. This is seen when Thomas questioned *"the way."* The thought here is the route, distance, mode, or means of getting to one's destination. Thomas may have had the assurance that he was going to heaven, but he was fearful of all that he must go through to get there. I must admit that the thoughts of suffering and problems do not generate excitement in my spirit, but most likely, these things are in my future. *"These things I have spoken unto you, that in me ye might have peace. In the world ye shall have tribulation: but be of good cheer; I have overcome the world" (John 16:33). "But the God of all grace, who hath called us unto his eternal glory by Christ Jesus, after that ye have suffered a while, make you perfect, stablish, strengthen, settle you" I Peter 5:10).* Jesus spoke of tribulation, and Peter points to suffering. Job's wife questioned the difficult times of life and encouraged her husband to take his own life. To this, Job responded by saying, *"Thou speakest as one of the foolish women speaketh. What? shall we receive good at the hand of God, and shall we not receive evil" (Job 2:10)?* David knew that the Lord would lead him in paths of righteousness, but he did not know what fields of adversity those paths would go through. Just as David had no knowledge of all that he would face in life, you and I find ourselves in the same position. But, this I do know, *"I will fear no evil: for thou art with me; thy rod and thy staff they comfort me" (Psalm 23:4).*

We, like Thomas, must deal with our fears of the future. There is the darkness of the future, the destination of the future, and the direction of the future. Ask the Lord to give peace about the direction He has in mind for your life, and submit to His sovereign will.

3. Fear of the Fantastic

Mary Magdalene lingered at the sepulchre weeping when Jesus revealed himself unto her *(see John 20:11-16).* After being comforted by her Lord, Mary returned to tell the disciples she had seen Him and to deliver His message to them. That evening, Jesus came and stood in midst of His disciples as they assembled for fear of the Jews. Thomas was missing from the group when the Lord first appeared unto them. When Thomas showed up, the other disciples told him that Jesus had appeared unto them. Thomas' response was, *"Except I shall see in his hands the print of the nails, and put my finger into the print of the nails, and thrust my hand into his side, I will not believe" (John 20:25).* Thomas had received word from Mary that Jesus was alive, and now, the other disciples are telling him that they have seen the risen Lord. Thomas doubted the **fantastic.** Thomas knew that Jesus had died on a Roman cross and had been laid to rest in a stone sepulchre. It was unreasonable to believe that Jesus had risen from the dead. A resurrected Lord would exceed human reasoning. It would be unbelievably great if Jesus had conquered death as He had said He would. Exceeds human reasoning, unbelievably great, these are but a few terms used to define fantastic. Yet, this is exactly what the Lord Jesus Christ did when He arose that third morning.

Like Thomas, many of us will not believe what we cannot experience with the five senses. When it comes to the fantastic, we are fearful. While I do know that there are those that make merchandise of the things of God, I am not going to let them scare me away from a Supernatural God. While I do not believe in divine healers, I do believe in the Great Physician. Because I am human, I have limitations, but I will not put limitation on my God. He can do abundantly above all that I ask or think. Whether it be the story of creation, the virgin birth, turning the water to wine, bringing Lazarus from the tomb, the Lord's resurrection on the third day, or any other miracles recorded in the Word of God, I believe it. May I be quick to add that my believing it does not give validity to truth. It is truth whether or not you or I believe it! God can and will do anything He wants!

Thomas said, "If I can see it, and feel it, I will believe." Jesus said, *"blessed are they that have not seen, and yet have believed" (John 20:29).* Our faith must be based upon His Word. It is faith in a God that can do anything that brings peace to the heart of His children.

Do you struggle with the same doubts as Thomas? Do you find yourself fearful of the foe, the future, and the fantastic? Cry out as I have to do so often, *"Lord . . . help thou mine unbelief."* May each of us respond to life with faith rather than with doubt.

Doubt's Results

There is a scientific law that states, "For every action, there is an opposite and equal reaction." God has a similar law that He has established. *"Be not deceived; God is not mocked: for whatsoever a man soweth, that shall he also reap" (Galatians 6:7).* If Thomas sows the seeds of doubt, he must reap the results of doubt! This principle is not only true for Thomas, it is true for everyone. If a sinner continually sows the seeds of doubt and will not accept the Lord Jesus Christ as his personal Saviour, the results are the eternal wrath of God. Just as there are results for doubt in the life of the sinner, there are results for doubt in the life of the believer. A believer with doubt. It almost sounds like a contradiction of terms, yet, Thomas was filled with doubt as so many of us are! Doubt is a very destructive force in the life of the believer. Faith brings life while doubt brings death. Thomas' doubt brought death to:

1. The Purpose of God

In *John 11*, Jesus was getting ready to return to Judaea to minister to the needs of His friends; Mary, Martha, and Lazarus. Jesus did not respond immediately to the news that Lazarus was sick. As a matter of fact, Jesus abode two days in the same place before He returned to Judaea. Did the absence of love for these folks cause Jesus to delay the return trip? No! The Bible is quick to point out that Jesus loved these individuals *(see verse 5)*. If it was not indifference or the absence of love, why did Jesus not respond immediately to the news and go to Judaea? Our Lord's supreme desire was to fulfill the purposes of God for His life. Jesus would go to Judaea when it was in accordance to the Father's will! While the Lord's faith would fulfill God's purposes, Thomas' doubt would destroy the **purposes of God** for his life.

If Jesus had allowed the doubt of Thomas and the other disciples to rule in this situation, the purposes of God would have been quenched in two areas. In responding to the news of Lazarus' sickness, Jesus said, *"This sickness is not unto death, but for the glory of God, that the Son of God might be glorified thereby"* *(verse 4)*. The first purpose in Lazarus' sickness was to **glorify God**. When Lazarus came forth from the grave at the command of Jesus, the Father would receive glory. The people would begin to praise God and worship Him for the great things He had done. At the same time, the Lord Jesus would be manifested as God, and glory would be ascribed to Him. Jesus would be praised, worshipped, and believed on by many of the Jews *(see verse 45)*. Doubt in the life of the believer does not glorify God; it diminishes God's glory before the eyes of others. Paul tells the believers at Corinth, *"For ye are bought with a price: therefore glorify God in your body, and in your spirit, which are God's"* *(I Corinthians 6:20)*. Listen to the words of Matthew, *"Let your* *light so shine before men, that they may see your good works, and glorify your Father which is in heaven" (Matthew 5:16).* As I examine my life, can I honestly say that I am bringing glory to my Heavenly Father? That is one area of God's will for each of us! The doubt in Thomas' life would destroy that purpose.

The trip to Judaea would reveal a second purpose, and that would be to **give life.** The Lord wants to reveal Himself as the God of the living and not of the dead *(see Mark 12:27).* While the Lord would give physical life to Lazarus, this miracle would serve as a beautiful type of God's plan of redemption. It is a picture of God giving life to the sinner dead in trespasses and sin. The Lord Jesus came for the express purpose to give His life that we may have life. Jesus said, *"I am come that they might have life, and that they might have it more abundantly" (John 10:10).* Listen to the statement of Thomas, *"Let us also go, that we may die with him" (John 11:16).* Be it the words of despondency or bravery, they are words that show nothing but the worst. Doubt caused Thomas to choose death over life. Once we have received new life in Christ, He wants us to enjoy not just life but abundant life. The word "abundantly" means superabundant in quantity and quality, in the sense of beyond. God does not require of us to be a dead sacrifice but rather a living sacrifice. *"I beseech you therefore, brethren, by the mercies of God, that ye present your bodies a living sacrifice, holy, acceptable unto God, which is your reasonable service. And be not conformed to this world: but be ye transformed by the renewing of your mind, that ye may prove what is that good, and acceptable, and perfect, will of God" (Romans 12:1-2).* Doubt keeps the believer from living life to its fullest for the honor and glory of God.

The doubt of Thomas would have destroyed the purposes of God if Christ had yielded to it. How many times has God's will and purposes been quenched because of our unbelief? In every situation of life, may we say with our Lord, *"Thy will be done."*

2. The Promise of God

When reading *John 14*, one must remember that very soon the Lord will be taken away. This event is something to which Jesus is trying to prepare the disciples. While finding it very disturbing, the disciples did not understand nor embrace this direction in the Lord's ministry. What method did Jesus use to help His disciples through this difficult time? Jesus left the disciples with the promises of God. He delivered to them the Word of God. Among the many other promises in *John 14,* Jesus told them of **a home, a hope,** and a **help**.

The Word of God is given to generate or encourage faith in the life of an individual. *"So then faith cometh by hearing, and hearing by the word of God" (Romans 10:17).* Faith can only be founded upon the Word of God! The doubt of Thomas was destructive and diminished the effectiveness of the **promises of God.** Faith rests upon the Word of God and attests to the validity of the truth while doubt rejects the Word of God and questions the reality of truth.

Jesus was concerned about the fear that had gripped the hearts of the disciples and wished to replace it with faith. Jesus said, *"Let not your heart be troubled" (John 14:1).* The word "troubled" means to stir or agitate the heart. Can you not see the contrast of fear and a troubled heart? What is the only thing that will dispel that fear? Do not miss the words of Jesus, *"believe also in me."* "Believe" means to have faith in or with respect to a person or thing, to trust one's spiritual well-being to Christ. The choice is yours, faith in the Word or continue to worry in fear.

Thomas' response to the words of Christ cast a shadow of doubt upon the promises of God. When someone looks at your life, does it encourage faith or reflect the fear that grips your troubled heart? Are you a living example of the truth of God's Word? Each of us is sowing seeds. Will you harvest fear or faith?

3. The Power of God

When the women and the disciples returned to the grave on the third day, they found it empty. The body had not been stolen as some would suggest, but He had risen victorious over death, hell, and the grave! This resurrected Lord manifested Himself unto Mary and some of the disciples that day *(see John 20:14&19)*. This appearance not only attested to the truth of God's Word, but it also spoke of the manifested power of God. Mary and the other disciples witnessed to Thomas. They told him of a Saviour that had power to get up out of the grave. It was a power that was sufficient to overcome the power of death. Thomas responded by saying, *"Except I shall see in his hands the print of the nails, and put my finger into the print of the nails, and thrust my hand into his side, I will not believe" (John 20:25)*. Doubt had rendered the **power of God** ineffective in the personal life of Thomas. Leslie Flynn said, "The real reason Thomas missed the meeting was he did not expect Jesus to be there. Thomas missed the presence of Christ, the teaching of the Word of God, the fellowship of believers, joy and peace, the commission of Christ, and seeing the wounds of Christ."

How many blessings have you missed out on because you rendered the power of God ineffective in your own personal life? The most prevalent example of this in each of our lives is in the area of prayer. James said, *"yet ye have not, because ye ask not" (James 4:2)*. We can try to explain away this verse, but the bottom line is we do not believe God is able to supply so we do not bother to even ask! Jesus told His disciples of a day coming in which they would accomplish great things. *"Verily, verily, I say unto you, He that believeth on me, the works that I do shall he do also; and greater works than these shall he do; because I go unto my Father" (John 14:12)*. The disciples would not only do the works of Christ, but they would do even greater things. This can only be accomplished through the power of God. How is one to harness this great power? By simply asking! *"And whatsoever ye shall ask in my name, that will I do, that the Father may be glorified in the Son. If ye shall ask any thing in my name, I will do it" (John 14:13-14).*

Faith is the key that places the power of God at our disposal. *"If ye have faith as a grain of mustard seed, ye shall say unto this mountain, Remove hence to yonder place; and it shall remove; and nothing shall be impossible unto you" (Matthew 17:20).* Doubt locks up God's power. Thomas did not harness the power of God; rather, he hindered its working in his own personal life.

When it comes to your own personal life, what has doubt destroyed for you, God's purpose, God's promise, or God's power? What things could have been accomplished if each of us would have responded in faith rather than fear? Remember, you can only harvest what you have sown!

Doubt's Removal

One does not have to be very spiritual to realize that Thomas had a real problem and the problem needed to be dealt with. Doubt is destroying the best that God has to offer His child. Faith had been driven from Thomas' heart by the battalion of fear. This warfare had left him weak and vulnerable to further attacks. In studying *John 20:19-31,* it becomes apparent that for eight days, Thomas had continued to dwell in doubt while the other disciples had rejoiced in faith at the sight of a resurrected Lord. The Lord had given them words of comfort and commission. Thomas' doubt had alienated him from the Lord and His people. The others were singing, "we have an anchor" as Thomas floundered in the midst of the storm. If Thomas was to be cured of this spiritual malady, doubt had to be removed from his heart! This would be easier said than done.

Can you relate to Thomas' condition? While you know that you are a member of the household of faith, you find yourself at a distance when it comes to the people of God. Faith comes so easy for them while your faith is challenged at every turn. The answer may appear too simplistic, but faith must replace the fear and the doubt that fills our heart if we are to experience recovery. How would this recovery be accomplished in Thomas' life? The answer is, a resurrected Lord must come to Thomas' aid! The compassion of God caused Him to move toward His needy children. Thomas did not seek out God, but the Lord comes to Thomas. What a blessing to my soul to know that this is the type of Saviour I have. God has always moved toward man when man was unable and unwilling to move toward God! "Hallelujah!" After eight days, the Lord returned to meet the needs of doubting Thomas. There were three things manifested in Thomas' meeting with the resurrected Lord.

1. The Confrontation with Faith

If doubt was to be driven from the heart of Thomas, there must have been a confrontation with faith. Since faith and fear cannot occupy the throne of one's heart, a battle must be waged and a victor crowned. We do not know the exact time Thomas joined the other disciples after the Lord's first visit, but eight days later, the Lord Jesus manifested Himself unto them a second time. Whatever the duration of time between Thomas joining them and the Lord's second appearance, the faith of the other disciples waged a war against Thomas' doubt. They rejoiced in belief while Thomas moaned in blindness. They voiced their confidence while Thomas vented his criticism. Everything that the other disciples found to establish their faith upon evaded the grasp of Thomas. If he was to embrace the truth they rested in, his doubt would have to yield in defeat. The resurrected Lord that had manifested Himself to them was manifesting Himself through them. Whether it be by words or works, their faith would not allow a truce to be called or negotiation for a peaceful settlement to continue. The demonstration of faith in the life of a believer is an affront to the doubt of another. Faith will settle for nothing short of total victory and domination!

It is one thing to have the faith of others waging war on the doubt that dwells within your heart, but then, the Lord manifests Himself. Upon revealing Himself, the Lord immediately confronted Thomas with these words, *"Reach hither thy finger, and behold my hands; and reach hither thy hand, and thrust it into my side: and be not faithless, but believing" (John 20:27).* This statement reveals the rebuke of the Lord! The Lord confronted Thomas with his doubt by using the word "faithless." The word means disbelieving, or without Christian faith, especially a heathen. Thomas professed to be a Christian while living like a heathen. Can you feel the embarrassment when the Lord told Thomas to touch and believe. The invitation to faith served as an indictment to doubt!

If you or I are to ever rid ourselves of doubt, there must be a confrontation with faith. This confrontation may come through the example of others or the invitation of the Saviour. In either case, only a war to the bitter end will yield a victor. May God be pleased to confront us with our doubts and fears that faith may flourish in our lives.

2. The Confession of Faith
Once the resurrected Lord had manifested Himself to Thomas and confronted him about his doubt, faith began to flourish in the heart of Thomas. This is evidenced by the confession of faith. *"And Thomas answered and said unto him, My Lord and my God" (John 20:28).* The first thing we can notice about this confession is that it was **personal.** Thomas said, *"My."* Try as he may, for nearly eight days, Thomas had been confronted by the faith of others, but it gave him no peace. Gaston Foote points out that there are two ways whereby men come to possess Christian faith. The first way is by inheritance. This comes to them by their parents, relatives, friends or associates. This is a secondhand faith. It may appear to be sufficient at first, but it will not stand the test of time. At some point, it will prove to be faulty because it is not personal. The only kind of faith that will suffice is personal faith. Gaston Foote said, "Men who possess a reliable practical faith are always those who, despite doubt and discouragement, put up a fight for it." Job knew this truth and said, *"But he knoweth the way that I take: when he hath tried me, I shall come forth as gold" (Job 23:10).* Peter also knew the

value of the truth in a personal way. Listen to what he was led by the Holy Spirit to say. *"That the trial of your faith, being much more precious than of gold that perisheth, though it be tried with fire, might be found unto praise and honour and glory at the appearing of Jesus Christ" (I Peter 1:7).* The quality of your faith is only known when it is tested, and only testing reveals if it is truly personal.

Thomas' confession of faith was not only personal, but it was in a **person,** *"My Lord and my God."* Thomas was no longer basing his faith on himself, human reason, or the faith of others, but upon the person of Christ. He confessed Christ to be very God of very God and to be the supreme authority and controller of all. There would be nothing enter the life of Thomas that his God was not sufficient to not only handle but was the master of it. With that kind of God, why worry or express any doubt for He is in control! A fuller knowledge and understanding of the character of God will yield faith and peace. Have you made any confessions of faith lately?

3. The Crown of Faith
While Thomas does make a confession of faith, the Lord tells about the crown of true faith. *"Jesus saith unto him, Thomas, because thou hast seen me, thou hast believed: blessed are they that have not seen, and yet have believed" (John 20:28).* The supremely blessed individual is that person that does not have full knowledge that comes from having a physical experience to base their trust in God. The supremely blessed may not understand it or know how God is going to do it, but they have faith in God's Word! Just the simple utterance of God is sufficient to place all confidence in God. If Thomas could have had this kind of confidence in Christ, he would not have been known as doubting Thomas.

The cure for the negative element of doubt is seeing a resurrected Lord *(John 20:28).* The positive response of faith is *"My Lord and my God!"* One cannot come into contact with the risen Lord and it not effect your life. The effect of the meeting with Christ was faithfulness in the life of Thomas. He missed the first meetings after the Lord's death, but He was there in the upper room faithful and obedient to the Lord's words *(see Acts 1:13)*. Thomas also proved to be faithful unto death. Thomas died a martyr's death, having been pierced by a lance in India. Leslie Flynn said, "The symbol for Thomas is a carpenter's square and a spear, because tradition says he erected a church with his own hands in the subcontinent of India to which he became a missionary and where he died a martyr, kneeling in prayer." Only a God could make such a difference in Thomas! Allow the resurrected Lord to generate faith in your heart. Do not sow the seeds of doubt because the fruit of the harvest is a bitter one. If doubt is detected in any degree in your heart, cry out unto the Lord and say, *"Help thou my unbelief."*

Chapter Ten

James and Judas, the Unnoticed Christians

Luke 6:13-16 "And when it was day, he called unto him his disciples: and of them he chose twelve, whom also he named apostles; Simon, (whom he also named Peter,) and Andrew his brother, James and John, Philip and Bartholomew, Matthew and Thomas, James the son of Alphaeus, and Simon called Zelotes, And Judas the brother of James, and Judas Iscariot, which also was the traitor."

James, the son of Alphaeus, and Judas, the brother of James, are the least known of all the apostles. One writer, in making reference to these two men, called them, "the obscure Apostles." J. Golden Burns said, "James and Judas are the prototypes of the unnumbered company throughout the ages who have lived and worked in the background, in whose case no amount of fidelity ever brought applause or even notice. If they teach anything, it is that honest service carries its own reward and that fame brings no real enhancement to man's worth, nor adds anything to his standing in the sight of God."

Judas is called Lebbaeus, whose surname was Thaddaeus *(see Matthew 10:3)*. Lebbaeus and Thaddaeus carry the idea "beloved," "warm hearted," or "full of heart;" thus courageous. The only direct reference to Judas in the Scriptures is when he asked a question in the upper room. *"Judas saith unto him, not Iscariot, Lord, how is it that thou wilt manifest thyself unto us, and not unto the world" (John 14:22)?* There is no record of James saying or doing anything individually. Since Matthew is referred to as the son of Alphaeus, it is likely that James and Matthew were brothers. It is thought that James and Judas were

118

Zealots, along with Simon.

With some individuals, God has chosen to record their works and not reveal their names. With James and Judas, God has chosen to record their names and not their labors. A close examination of each group will reveal that while certain things differ about the two groups, there is one common element of truth; both were unnoticed by the world! Because of this central truth, there are certain principles that hold true to both groups. It is only by looking simultaneously at those with no recorded name and those with no recorded labor that the zenith of these principles can be understood. This collective group were the unnoticed Christians.

Unnoticed, But Not Unseen!

Webster points out that the word "unnoticed" conveys the thought of not making mention of or reference to, not given attention or heeded, to fail to observe. It was not the fact that James and Judas failed to be present when great events took place, it was that no one took the trouble to see if they were there! The names of James and Judas were never referred to or mentioned by those that desired to crush the works of Christ. The world at large failed to observe the absence or the presence of these men. It is as if these men never even existed.

While it appears that James and Judas were unnoticed, one must remember they were not unseen! *"For the eyes of the Lord are over the righteous, and his ears are open unto their prayers" (I Peter 3:12). "For the ways of man are before the eyes of the LORD, and he pondereth all his goings" (Proverbs 5:1). "The eyes of the LORD are in every place, beholding the evil and the good" (Proverbs 15:3).*

You may perceive yourself to be very much like James and Judas. You may be thinking to yourself, "Nobody even knows I'm alive!" You may see yourself as Moses, hid on the backside of the desert, pastoring in a place that you cannot get there from here. You may be hid in the Sunday School department with a class that no one wants and where nothing appears to be happening. You see yourself in the shadows doing menial labor while others appear before the crowds soaking up the bright lights. Your name is only mentioned in the sentence, "I didn't know they were members of the church." Just remember, you may appear to be unnoticed by the world and Christianity at large, but you are not unseen. There is one from whose presence you can never escape. David said, *"Whither shall I go from thy spirit? or whither shall I flee from thy presence? If I ascend up into heaven, thou art there: if I make my bed in hell, behold, thou art there. If I take the wings of the morning, and dwell in the uttermost parts of the sea; Even there shall thy hand lead me, and thy right hand shall hold me. If I say, Surely the darkness shall cover me; even the night shall be light about me. Yea, the darkness hideth not from thee; but the night shineth as the day: the darkness and the light are both alike to thee. For thou hast possessed my reins: thou hast covered me in my mother's womb"* *(Psalm 139:7-13).*

What was it that placed James and Judas among the unnoticed and others in the light of popularity? What does it take to catch the eye of the public? Why am I among the obscure? The answer to these questions may be found in the lives of those with recorded labors and no name!

The day was far spent, and the mass of people had not eaten. Jesus tells the disciples to feed the crowd. As they ponder the need and search for a source of supply, the answer is standing among them. The reason the small boy went unnoticed to the majority was the **portion** he had to offer. *"There is a lad here, which hath five barley loaves, and two small fishes: but what are they among so many" (John 6:9)?* The attitude of the disciples was, "The size of the crowd is so large, and the lad has so little!" The lad was given little attention by those actively trying to do the Lord's work. Both the disciples and the Lord were looking at the quantity the lad had to offer. The difference was the perspective each took. The disciples said, "How much can the lad give?" The Lord said, "How much will the lad have left?" The world did not notice the boy because he did not have a lot to give, but the lad caught the eye of God because he had given his all.

You may feel like you do not have a lot to offer. You are not prolific in your speech, have not the abundance of wealth, and not given to an outgoing personality, but have you given the Lord all? Whatever the size of your gift, it has not escaped the eye of the Saviour.

The Lord Jesus has taken a seat over against the treasury and is watching the giving of the people. A lone figure walks up and drops in two mites, which make a farthing. Neither the priests of the temple nor the Lord's disciples acknowledged the giver. Was the giver unnoticed because of her gender or the fact that she was a widow *(see Mark 12:41-44)*? No! She was unnoticed to those about her because of the **praise** attributed to the giving of others. In *Matthew 6:1-3,* we have a description of the method in which most of the giving took place in the days of our Lord. The rich would make their way to the treasury dressed in their finest apparel. Preceding them would be servants carrying elaborate gifts for all to view. In addition, there would be the sounding of a trumpet to announce to all that great gifts were being brought by some notable person. Desiring to please her God rather than gain the praise of men, the widow silently slipped into the treasury and gave all that she had. Jesus said of those that give to gain the attention of men, *"They have their reward" (Matthew 6:2).*

You may be a bi-vocational preacher that gives every minute of your free time to the work of the ministry. You minister to a group that is smaller than the average Sunday school class. Religious potentates do not know you at denominational headquarters. Your name has not appeared in any religious periodicals. You are hardly noticed by the brethren. You silently give all to please the Saviour. While you are unnoticed by "them," rejoice in the fact that you are seen of "Him."

You may run a bus in the part of town no one else will take. Others have tried on numerous occasions to build a route only to yield to defeat. Every week, as regular as the earth rotates on its axis, you have knocked on every door. Not one time have you been honored as bus route of the week. Take comfort dear friend, He has seen your sacrifice.

Jesus received an invitation from a Pharisee to sit at meat with him. Accepting the invitation, Jesus entered into the home and reclines at the table. Moving out of the darkness of the street, a woman enters the room. Without hesitation, she went straight for the Son of God. Taking a place at the feet of the Saviour, she begins to lavish upon Him precious ointment from an alabaster box *(see Luke 7:36-39)*. The cost of her devotion is unnoticed to those about the table because of a **past** that haunts her. Rather than seeing her gift, they were consumed with her guilt. They could not rejoice in the present for rehashing the past. Jesus himself faced similar criticism in reference to His past. *"Is not this the carpenter's son? is not his mother called Mary? and his brethren, James, and Joses, and Simon, and Judas? And his sisters, are they not all with us? Whence then hath this man all these things? And they were offended in him" (Matthew 13:55-57).*

The crowded room of Pharisees gave no attention to the new creature in Christ because of the cruelty of their own heart. They had forgotten that the blood covers it all! There are numerous individuals that must relocate in order to minister. Many have received the forgiveness of God but not the forgiveness of society. There are some cases where the Christian lives long enough to prove a change has taken place, but it is difficult.

The treasure in her hand, the tears in her eyes, and the tenderness of her heart went unnoticed to those that were obsessed with the sins of her past rather than the salvation of the present! The Pharisee's eyes were closed to the present and open to the past, while the Lord's eyes are closed to the past and open to the present!

James and Judas received little or no attention from those about them. These men are not mentioned to any degree in the writings of the early church fathers. Most preachers do not use these men as a point of reference or encourage their people to follow in their footsteps. Neither the world nor Christianity has given much attention to James or Judas. Yet, when one is unnoticed by others, it is imperative to remember we never escape the eye of God. There is one that knows and cares!

Unnoticed, But Not Unneeded!

James and Judas lived lives that were obscure. These men went through life relatively unnoticed by anyone around them, but it does not mean that their lives were without meaning or purpose! Remember this verse, *"And when it was day, he called unto him his disciples: and of them he chose twelve, whom also he named apostles" (Luke 6:13)*. James and Judas were hand picked by the Lord Jesus Christ to be apostles. These two unnoticed Christians were just as needed in the plans and purposes of God as Peter, John, or any of the other apostles! We do not have recorded for us all the ways in which the Lord used James and Judas during His earthly ministry. In many places, when referring to a task, the Scriptures say, *"he sent two of his disciples" (see Luke 19:29)*. Names of those that performed the services for the Saviour are sometimes omitted. It may have been James and Judas that sought out the colt for the Lord's triumphal entry into Jerusalem. We do know that on two occasions James and Judas helped feed a multitude of people *(see John 6 & Matthew 15)*.

While many Christians are unnoticed, there are numerous purposes for which God chooses to use them. A close look at the unnamed servants reveal several purposes of God.

Jesus instructs the apostles to have the people sit down in companies *(see Mark 6:39)*. He then took the small portion of five barley loaves and two small fishes from the young lad. The boy may have been unnoticed, but he was needed to reveal the **Power of God** and the **Person of Christ** *(John 6:14)*. Committing everything into the hands of Jesus, the lad placed at Jesus' disposal a means by which the Lord revealed a power that could only be attributed to God. With that lunch, Jesus would feed five thousand men plus the women and children. After everyone had eaten, twelve baskets of fragments were taken up. Only God could take so little and do so much! This is exactly what all those that had witnessed the miracle performed by Jesus had said. *"Then those men, when they had seen the miracle that Jesus did, said, This is of a truth that prophet that should come into the world" (John 6:14).* The men realized that Jesus was the one promised and spoken of in the Scriptures. All this was accomplished because someone unnoticed by the world was willing to place all of their small portion into the hands of the Saviour. You may be unnoticed, but you can serve His purpose!

The trumpet was blasting as the long procession of servants passed carrying the elaborate gifts of the rich. All eyes were upon the individual dressed in the finest apparel as the widow silently dropped in two mites *(Mark 12:42)*. She may have been unnoticed by others, but she was needed to reveal the **Perception of God**. While others saw the elaborate gifts, Jesus perceived the emptiness of their giving. *"For the LORD seeth not as man seeth; for man looketh on the outward appearance, but the LORD looketh on the heart" (I Samuel 16:7).* Jesus was aware that most giving was for a demonstration rather than evidence of devotion. Jesus pointed out to the disciples that the gift of the widow was more than all the other gifts combined. *"Verily I say unto you, That this poor widow hath cast more in, than all they which have cast into the treasury" (Mark 12:43).* Jesus knows the heart of each one of us. He knows when we give, why we give, and how much we give. If we are to honor Christ, we must give Him all. We must be sure to remember that what is brought in the hand is representative of what's in the heart. While others may not see or know, God does!

There is a coldness in the room as the woman stoops at the feet of Jesus. Tears flow from her cheeks as precious ointment flows from the alabaster box. In the sight of God, the tears are of more value than the ointment. While the religious Pharisees would have driven her into the street, Jesus would have her there for He needed her to reveal the **Pardon of God**. Jesus was not minimizing this woman's sin but rather maximizing the salvation of God. Listen to the words of our Lord, *"Wherefore I say unto thee, Her sins, which are many, are forgiven; for she loved much" (Luke 7:47)*. Paul emphasized this same truth when making reference to himself. *"This is a faithful saying, and worthy of all acceptation, that Christ Jesus came into the world to save sinners; of whom I am chief" (I Timothy 1:15)*. God used this sinful woman to reveal that while one's past may be bad, their future can be bright! Why? Because of the abundant and sufficient pardon of the Lord.

We have not been given all the tasks in which the Lord used James and Judas. These men may have had little to give, a sorted past to overcome, and been hidden beneath the praises of other men, but God needed them and chose them. Why would God choose such men as James and Judas? One possibility is that God used them for their absence of talent and ability rather than their abundance. God's choice of servants is controlled by what He already knows. *"For ye see your calling, brethren, how that not many wise men after the flesh, not many mighty, not many noble, are called: But God hath chosen the foolish things of the world to confound the wise; and God hath chosen the weak things of the world to confound the things which are mighty; And base things of the world, and things which are despised, hath God chosen, yea, and things which are not, to bring to nought things that are: That no flesh should glory in his presence" (I Corinthians 1:26-29)*. The omniscience of God reveals that ultimate glory is brought to God when great things are accomplished through weak things rather than mighty things. You may be unnoticed, but it does not mean that you cannot be used to bring maximum glory to God. Try giving God all!

Unnoticed, But Not Unrewarded!

James and Judas did not catch the eye of those about them. There were no reports of these men doing extraordinary works among the general populace. There was no delegation sent out by main stream religion, as they did with John the Baptist, to investigate who these men were *(see John 1:19)*. James and Judas quietly stood in the shadows and served the Lord at every given opportunity. God had a perfect will for each of the men, and each submitted to be used where the Lord placed them. While their service was unnoticed by most, it will not go unrewarded by the Saviour. *"For God is not unrighteous to forget your work and labour of love, which ye have showed toward his name, in that ye have ministered to the saints, and do minister" (Hebrews 6:10). "For the Son of man shall come in the glory of his Father with his angels; and then he shall reward every man according to his works" (Matthew 16:27).* No one's labors will go unnoticed or unrewarded. There will be a day coming when all will be made manifest, and these obscure servants of the Lord will be honored before the host of heaven.

To what degree will James and Judas be rewarded? In order to answer this question, I want to look again at the other unnamed and unnoticed individuals in the Bible.

As the mass of people followed the Lord out into the countryside, they began to be fatigued and hungry. They had been with Him most of the day and had eaten nothing. To meet the need of the hour, there was a young lad with five barley loaves and two small fishes. The only two people that noticed him was Jesus and Andrew. While unnoticed, he placed into the hands of the Lord all that he had. The bread was most likely in the shape of small hearth cakes, and the fish was salted or dried. One must remember that it was an amount equal to a boy's lunch. While it may have been small, it was all that he had, and the lad would be rewarded. After the people were fed, Jesus sent the disciples back around. This trip, they were not to give but to receive *(see John 6:12)*. They gathered up the fragments from the five loaves and two small fishes, an amount consisting of twelve baskets filled to capacity. The young lad was rewarded with **physical riches.** Can you not imagine the look on the young lad's face when Jesus returned to him the unused portion? What do you think his parents thought when he returned to the house with such a large amount of food? While the investment was so small, the rewards were so great!

After the rich young ruler rejected Christ for the love of riches, Peter spoke up and said, *"Lo, we have left all, and have followed thee" (Mark 10:28).* Peter wanted to know what would be his reward for turning his back on the world so that he might follow Christ. In response to this question, Jesus said, *"Verily I say unto you, There is no man that hath left house, or brethren, or sisters, or father, or mother, or wife, or children, or lands, for my sake, and the gospel's, But he shall receive an hundredfold now in this time" (Mark 10:29-30).* Jesus tells Peter that in addition to eternal life, there was physical riches amounting to one hundred fold in this present world. It pays to serve the Lord now. There are earthly rewards for those who commit all to Him. The Christian life is a blessed life. James and Judas were being rewarded daily for serving their Lord and Saviour and so are you. David said, *"I have been young, and now am old; yet have I not seen the righteous forsaken, nor his seed begging bread" (Psalm 37:25).* God rewards those that serve Him!

In humility, the woman with the sorted past bowed at the feet of Jesus. Not one word flowed across her lips, but her actions spoke volumes. The only thing stronger than the sweet smell of that precious ointment is the love that flowed from her heart. While others seek to ridicule, the Lord Jesus means to reward. This act of devotion will be rewarded with a **permanent record.** *"Verily I say unto you, Wheresoever this gospel shall be preached in the* *whole world, there shall also this, that this woman hath done, be told for a memorial of her" (Matthew 26:13).* Jesus tells us that this act of devotion will never be forgotten. It does not matter whether the gift or service be great or small, it will be rewarded. This truth can be seen in the words of our Lord when He said, *"And whosoever shall give to drink unto one of these little ones a cup of cold water only in the name of a disciple, verily I say unto you, he shall in no wise lose his reward" (Matthew 10:42).*

For every individual, both saved and lost, there is a permanent record being kept! For the lost, they will appear at the great white throne judgment. *"And I saw the dead, small and great, stand before God; and the books were opened: and another book was opened, which is the book of life: and the dead were judged out of those things which were written in the books, according to their works" (Revelation 20:12).* This judgment is not to determine whether the individual is saved or lost but the degrees of punishment for the way they lived. Everything is recorded in the books! There will be nothing missed in that day.

Those that are saved will appear before the judgment seat of Christ. *"Every man's work shall be made manifest: for the day shall declare it, because it shall be revealed by fire; and the fire shall try every man's work of what sort it is. If any man's work abide which he hath built thereupon, he shall receive a reward. If any man's work shall be burned, he shall suffer loss: but he himself shall be saved; yet so as by fire" (I Corinthians 3:13-15).* Paul points out that the method for testing our works is fire, and the motive for the test is to determine the nature and quality of our works. Those works that stand the test of the fire will bring us a reward.

"But I say unto you, That every idle word that men shall speak, they shall give account thereof in the day of judgment" (Matthew 12:36). There will be nothing missed at either judgment! Nothing! At which judgment will you appear? If you do not know the Lord Jesus Christ as your personal Saviour,

why not bow your head and ask Him to save you right now? God is keeping a permanent record!

The little widow silently dropped in two mites and was quickly lost in the crowd. Jesus watched as all the givers paraded by. Some gained the attention of those about the offering bins, but only one impressed the Son of God. The religious clamor and pharisaical side show had nauseated the Lord Jesus. The applause and fanfare heaped upon the proud individual is their reward. *"Therefore when thou doest thine alms, do not sound a trumpet before thee, as the hypocrites do in the synagogues and in the streets, that they may have glory of men. Verily I say unto you, They have their reward"* (Matthew 6:2).

Looking over the entire crowd of givers, Jesus singled out one to be rewarded. While the others are rewarded with the temporal praises of men, the widow was rewarded with a **potentate's recognition.** *"And he called unto him his disciples, and saith unto them, Verily I say unto you, That this poor widow hath cast more in, than all they which have cast into the treasury: For all they did cast in of their abundance; but she of her want did cast in all that she had, even all her living"* (Mark 12:43-44). The King of Kings lavished upon that lowly widow eternal praises for her gifts unto God! From whom will you receive your praise? It is the desire of my heart to hear my Lord say, *"Well done, good and faithful servant; thou hast been faithful over a few things, I will make thee ruler over many things: enter thou into the joy of thy lord"* (Matthew 25:23). I would rather know that I have pleased Him than to have the applause of the whole world.

James and Judas were unnoticed by those about them. The little lad, the woman with the sorted past, and the widow received little or no recognition from the world. While individuals may be unnoticed, each of us will be rewarded. The Lord said, *"And, behold, I come quickly; and my reward is with me, to give every man according as his work shall be"* (Revelation 22:12). It is worth noting that the word "reward," which means pay or wages for service, can be good or bad. The reward may be riches, or it may be wrath. What type of rewards will you have?

Unnoticed, But Not Unfaithful!

In many cases, those that do not receive the applause of the world generally quit. This was not the case with James and Judas. They may have been unnoticed, but these men were faithful unto death! J.D. Jones said, "These men are a rebuke to most of us. The hard thing is to do one's best when no one watches, and no one notices, and no one praises." These men did not allow their lack of publicity to smother their faithful and consistent life for Christ.

While there is some disagreement as to the exact way these men died, it is agreed that both suffered sacrificial deaths for the cause of Christ! It was told that James was thrown from the temple by the scribes and Pharisees. He was then stoned, and his brains dashed out by a fuller's club. It is thought that Judas died in some similar form of sacrificial death.

Neither of these men turned their back on the Saviour. They placed all on the altar for the cause of Christ. As you look at your commitment, how does it compare with these unnoticed Christians?

James and Judas were obscure men! They did not get the attention of the world, nor the applause of the religious community. Unnoticed? Yes, but not unseen! God's eye was upon every move they made or didn't make. These men were needed in the ministry of our Lord and Saviour Jesus Christ. He handpicked them to serve, and He is going to reward them for their labors of love. It was love that kept them faithfully serving the Lamb of God. You may be unnoticed, but you can be encouraged by the fact that God is watching and has a place of service for each of us. For those that remain faithful, there will be a reward in this life and in the world to come! May these men's words and works serve as an admonishment to each of us.

Chapter Eleven

Simon, the Zealous Christian

Matthew 10:4 "Simon the Canaanite" Mark 3:18 "Simon the Canaanite"
Luke 6:15 "Simon called Zelotes" Acts 1:13 "And when they were come in, they went up into an upper room, where abode both Peter, and James, and John, and Andrew, Philip, and Thomas, Bartholomew, and Matthew, James the son of Alphaeus, and Simon Zelotes"

Simon is only mentioned four times in the Word of God, but every time his name is associated with one overshadowing truth, he was "zealous." In two passages that mention his name, the word "Canaanite" is used. This word is not a geographical term but is derived from a Hebrew word which means "to be ardent or zealous." The second term, used in the other two passages, is the word "Zelotes." Both "Canaanite" and "Zelotes" have reference to a political party known as the Zealots. Webster defines the term as "patriotism, love, and loyal or zealous support of one's own country." Emerging as one of the last great Jewish parties, they were a group of fervent patriots. They would use any means or method necessary to free their country from the grip of Roman domination, even bloodshed. They viewed their cause not so much a political insurrection but as a holy war.

All that we know of Simon was that he was a Zealot, and he is not to be confused with Simon who is called Peter. Listen to the words of William McIntyre, "His personal characteristic was zeal. One needs to understand what Jewish patriotism really meant. In a peculiar sense it was patriotism for the Kingdom of God. The people believed that the kingdom of Judea and the

131

Kingdom of God were interchangeable." While it is dangerous to build a whole sermon on one word, I have heard some built on a lot less. The fact that Simon was a Zealot tells us a great deal about him. We know some of his beliefs and to what length he would go to secure them. It tells us that he had priorities and a value system in his life.

It was God's marvelous Grace that was able to transfer Simon's zeal from that of a physical temporal kingdom, to a Spiritual eternal kingdom. It was Jesus Christ who enabled Simon to drop the sword of insurrection and pick up the sword of the Spirit. Simon's zeal was not diminished, only redirected toward the things of God. Where is the focus of your zeal directed? What are the priorities in your life? What kind of value system do you have?

Blending what we know about Simon and the principles of Scripture concerning the subject of zeal, I want to investigate the zealous Christian. Together, may we find out those things that make up such an individual, contrast them with our personal relationship with God, and emulate these attributes in our lives.

The Character of a Zealous Christian

It is imperative to have an understanding of this band of freedom fighters named Zealots if one is to understand the character of a zealous Christian. The Zealots were established some twenty years before Jesus began his public ministry. The Zealot was a patriot that was willing to draw his sword for his country and if need be, to die for its deliverance. When the Roman government instituted a census for the purpose of taxation, the Zealots immediately led a revolt. God was the only king, and the only one to whom tribute should be paid. These Jewish rebels were zealous for the Law and bitterly hated the domination of a foreign power. Josephus said of them, "They (the Zealots) have an inviolable attachment to liberty and say that God is their only Ruler and Lord. They do not mind dying any kind of death, nor do they heed the torture of their kindred and friends, nor can any such fear make them call any man lord."

It was this strong will and devotion that God harnessed and directed in the life of Simon. The one devoted to a country became devoted to Christ. There are several characteristics that mark those belonging to the Zealots.

1. Zeal

The dictionary defines zeal as to be filled with enthusiasm, the strong excitement of feeling or its cause. It requires little or no imagination to perceive that zeal was the chief characteristic of a Zealot. A Zealot could not talk about foreign oppression without his blood pressure rising along with voice. If you did not want a verbal tongue lashing you had better not oppose his view. He did not feel the least bit backwards in expressing his feelings on the affairs of state. His zeal would cause him to rise in the middle of the night to strike revenge at Rome under the cover of darkness. The Zealot lived for the privilege of crushing the enemy and was on guard for any opportunity that presented itself to do so.

Where is the evidence of strong feelings toward the things of God in the average believer's life? Why can we get mad enough to fight when someone criticizes our political candidate while calmly standing by as they take the name of the Lord in vain? We have no problem becoming very vocal over social views, but when it comes to witnessing for Christ, we are like an arctic river, frozen at the mouth. God said, *"Let the redeemed of the LORD say so, whom he hath redeemed from the hand of the enemy" (Psalm 107:2)*. We readily welcome being called a *fan* for a sports figure but fear the reprisal of being call a *fanatic* for the Saviour. *"The fear of man bringeth a snare: but whoso putteth his trust in the LORD shall be safe" (Proverbs 29:25)*.

Zeal will drive us into the woods before daylight on opening morning of hunting season, while we lay in a comatose state on Sunday morning, contemplating the sacrifice that will be involved in making the morning worship. Should we just lie there and make an effort to go next week? With the baby in tow, we walk from the far end of the mall parking lot to spend the day catching all the bargains of the season, but revival is out of the question because it's too much trouble. We go an hour early to meet with a school club, give up our lunch period to practice for a play, stay over for two hours of basketball practice, but you want me to give an hour on Sunday evening to come to the youth meeting? You must be out of your mind!

Where is the Christian zeal that liberates our tongue, makes proper use of our time, and makes available our talents for the glory of God? It is not that we are a people void of zeal, only a people with misplaced zeal.

2. Unity

Unity is a strong characteristic of a Zealot. It would be unthinkable for one Zealot to sellout another. The love for country and freedom bound them together with a bond stronger than blood. This bond would cause them to dismiss social, physical, and sexual barriers for the common cause of country. Unity would be maintained at any cost!

In Simon's life, there was now a cause that superseded that of the Zealots! Where his allegiance had once been to a country, now it was to Christ, and the principle of unity was still in force. As one reads the list of the twelve, it becomes apparent that there were two men in this company that hold opposite political views. Simon is a Zealot, while Matthew is a turncoat. One would die for the cause of liberty, and the other is selling his own people into greater bondage. Previous to these men meeting the Lord Jesus Christ, Simon would have taken the life of Matthew with no remorse. Now the story is different! Both now rally under the banner of love. They are now bound by the same goal as they fight the common enemy of sin. Each has come to realize that man's need is not liberty in one's country but liberty in Christ.

Is there unity within the body of Christ today? Jesus said, *"By this shall all men know that ye are my disciples, if ye have love one to another" (John 13:35).* The church at Corinth was marked by division. Writing to them Paul said, *"Now I beseech you, brethren, by the name of our Lord Jesus Christ, that ye all speak the same thing, and that there be no divisions among you; but that ye be perfectly joined together in the same mind and in the same judgment" (I Corinthians 1:10).* The Corinthian believers clung to personalities, but the zealous Christian clings to the person of Christ. Thirteen times in the New Testament, God gives encouragement to *"love one another."*

3. Faithfulness

A Zealot was characterized by faithfulness. The decision to become a Zealot was not one to be taken lightly. It was not something that one joined for a year or two and then got out because of a lack of interest. These rebel patriots were faithful even to death, both theirs and those of their family.

Simon's life was characterized by faithfulness. Just as God would transform Matthew's pen, He would transform Simon's loyalty. If one was to disregard the traitor Judas from the list of the Apostles, then Simon would appear last or next to last in every list. Yet, he remained faithful. Every time the Apostles are mentioned collectively, Simon is there. This cannot be said of Thomas or Judas.

As a zealous Christian, Paul possessed faithfulness. Listen to one of his statements of faithfulness, *"Brethren, I count not myself to have apprehended: but this one thing I do, forgetting those things which are behind, and reaching forth unto those things which are before, I press toward the mark for the prize of the high calling of God in Christ Jesus" (Philippians 3:13-14).* As the chief attributes are listed for the stewards of the Lord, faithfulness is listed as supreme *(see I Corinthians 4:2).* Are we faithful to our Lord and Saviour Jesus Christ?

The characteristics that made Simon a Zealot, *zeal*, *unity*, and *faithfulness*, were not extinguished by the Lord Jesus when Simon became an apostle; they were redirected and enhanced for the glory of God. The Zealot became a zealous Christian. As one inventories their life, the attributes of zeal, unity, and faithfulness will be found. What one must ask themselves is, to whom are these attributes directed, self, Satan, or the Saviour?

The Cost of being a Zealous Christian

When a man chose to become a Zealot, there was no price he was not willing to pay to drive the oppressors from country and secure his objective. Listen to the words of James Golder Burns when speaking of the Zealots, "They had a loathing hatred of the foreigners and grim resolve to sacrifice everything, even life itself, to bring his detested supremacy to an end." Please note the phrase, "resolve to sacrifice everything."

Simon had been willing to sacrifice all for his country, and now, Simon was willing to sacrifice all for Christ. While salvation is the free gift of God, there is sacrificial cost if one is to become a zealous Christian! There are two areas I want to examine as one thinks of cost.

1. Expectation

There is a misconception among many today that God does not expect the believer to sacrifice anything. God is perceived as so loving that any level of devotion excites the heart of God. God is so hard up for individuals to follow Him that a tip of the hat and a dollar in the plate will make God your humble servant. If this is your mentality, you don't know God. God is a God of expectations! Once an individual is a recipient of grace, God expects us to yield totally and completely in every area of our lives.

While eating bread on the Sabbath day with one of the chief Pharisees and the lawyers, one replied, *"Blessed is he that shall eat bread in the kingdom of God" (Luke 14:15).* Jesus responded with a parable telling who would make up the kingdom of God, and then, He turned to the great multitude that was following Him and said, *"If any man come to me, and hate not his father, and mother, and wife, and children, and brethren, and sisters, yea, and his own life also, he cannot be my disciple" (Luke 14:26)*. The expectation of God is total **devotion**. The word "hate" means to detest, especially to persecute, to be loveless. God will not be relegated to a subordinate place in your life. If one is to be His disciple, there can be no rival for the love He is due. Who or what occupies first place in your life?

Jesus was alone praying with His disciples when He asked them, *"Whom say the people that I am" (Luke 9:18)*? From this question, Jesus reveals His person, *"The Christ of God"* and His purpose, *"suffer . . . rejected . . . be slain . . . raised the third day" (vs. 20&22)*. Having thus done, Jesus turns to His disciples *"And he said to them all, If any man will come after me, let him deny himself, and take up his cross daily, and follow me" (vs. 23)*. It was the purpose of Christ to yield to the cross, and His expectations for those that were His disciples was to yield **self** to the cross. There were to be no exceptions, for the statement was given to all, *"And he said to them all."* The sacrifice of self is not just for the preacher, the deacon, the teacher, the youth workers, the missionary, but for all. We not only see the magnitude of the sacrifice, *"all,"* but also the timing of the sacrifice, *"daily."* The cross was an instrument of death. The expectation of God is that all of us daily yield self to the cross of Christ that we might die and He might live in and out of us.

When writing to the believers at Rome, Paul said, *"I beseech you therefore, brethren, by the mercies of God, that ye present your bodies a living sacrifice, holy, acceptable unto God, which is your reasonable service" (Romans 12:1)*. The expectation of God is to use our hands, our lips, our eyes, our feet, our **body** for the performance of His will on this earth. When Jesus was on this earth, He said, *"I am,"* and in preparation for leaving, He said, *"ye are" (John 8:12 & Matthew 5:14)*.

The expectations of God are very high, but they seem so small when one considers the monumental cost He was willing to pay for sinful men.

2. Examples

We have, throughout the Word of God, examples of believers that were willing to pay the cost to be a zealous Christian.

There is the devotion of Mary in *Matthew 26*. Mary brings a precious ointment in an alabaster box and pours it out upon the head of the Lord Jesus Christ. The cost of the precious ointment was a year's wages. Mary is giving more than just a portion of her monetary means; this offering is representative of the giving of herself totally and completely unto the Lord. Mary could have sung with the great hymn writer, Frances Havergal, "Take my life, and let it be consecrated Lord to Thee, Take my feet, and let them be swift and beautiful for Thee, Take my lips, and let them be filled with messages for Thee. Take my love, my God, I pour at Thy feet its treasure store."

The apostle Paul was one that was willing to pay the cost! He placed an offering of his body upon the altar of God. When writing to the Corinthian believers in *II Corinthians 11*, Paul spoke of that offering. He said in *verse 23, "Are they ministers of Christ? (I speak as a fool) I am more; in labours more abundant, in stripes above measure, in prisons more frequent, in deaths oft."* He was stoned and left for dead outside the city at Lystra. He was beaten on numerous occasions. Paul yielded his body for the cause of Christ.

When we think of paying the cost of being a zealous Christian, might we ask the question of the songwriter, Thomas Shepherd, "Must Jesus bear the cross alone, and all the world go free?" Will we be too cheap and selfish to pay the cost, or will we answer in the affirmative, "No; there's a cross for every one, and there's a cross for me?"

The Call to be a Zealous Christian

God wanted all of His children to be zealous Christians. Paul sent a letter to a young man named Titus, a son in the faith, to give directions as to how to live in this present world. In chapter one, Paul instructs Titus. In chapter two, Paul instructs men, women, servants, and also speaks to them collectively as the body of Christ. I want to draw your attention to *verse 14, "Who gave himself for us, that he might redeem us from all iniquity, and purify unto himself a peculiar people, zealous of good works."* The Lord Jesus went to the cross that He might redeem us from what we were and make of us what He wanted, *"a peculiar people, **zealous of good works**."* The word Paul used, "zealous," and the word used to describe Simon, "Zelotes," is the same word. Are we living up to our purpose? God's people are to be beyond the usual *(study the word "peculiar").* Our efforts, acts, and deeds are to be valuable and virtuous in appearance or use.

In another one of Paul's writings, we are told, *"And whatsoever ye do, do it heartily, as to the Lord, and not unto men" (Colossians 3:23).* We are admonished to serve our Saviour heartily. When writing to the Laodiceans in *Revelation 3,* God was upset with their lukewarm state. They were neither hot nor cold, but lukewarm. Are we not living in the Laodicean church age? Where is our zeal, our hearty service, and our fire for God? You do not have to answer for the church collectively. I do not have to answer for the church collectively. But, I do have to give an account for myself. Am I a zealous Christian?

All of us would have to agree from the Word of God that God has called us to be zealous Christians. As we think of being a zealous Christian, there are two areas that we need to consider.

1. The Course of Zeal

It is one thing to have zeal, it is another to have it directed in the right direction or for the right purpose. Simon had zeal previous to meeting the Lord Jesus Christ, but it was focused on the wrong thing. Speaking of himself, Paul spoke of a misdirected zeal in *Galatians 1:14, "And profited in the Jews' religion above many my equals in mine own nation, being more exceedingly zealous of the traditions of my fathers."* Paul excelled above all those about him in the Jewish religion, but his zeal was not directed toward Christ. So many of those that are caught up in cults are very zealous, but they know not the true and living God. They ride bicycles throughout town, pass out literature from door to door, give a year of their life to serve, and yet know not the Lord Jesus Christ in the free pardon of sin. It is the case of a misdirected zeal.

When writing to the church at Rome, Paul spoke of the zeal of ignorance. *"For I bear them record that they have a zeal of God, but not according to knowledge. For they being ignorant of God's righteousness, and going about to establish their own righteousness, have not submitted themselves unto the righteousness of God" (Romans 10:2-3).* When I think of this kind of zeal, I am reminded of a story by Dr. Curtis Hutson. An airplane left Los Angeles for Hawaii. After a couple of hours, the zealous pilot announced, "I am sorry to inform you that we are lost. However, we are making good time." The believers at Rome had zeal, but they lacked full discernment when it came to the things of God. They were satisfied with religious emotion and activity, even if it contained no truth. They were like the zealous pilot, give me activity, even if it is in the wrong direction. Is what we are doing moving us, and those to whom we are ministering, toward Christ and the things of God because our zeal is coupled with discernment? The only way to assure this is stay in the Scriptures and be lead of the Spirit!

2. The Contagiousness of Zeal
At most sporting events, there is a small group of individuals, just off the field of play, known as cheerleaders. Why are they there? What purpose could they possibly serve? This small group is to generate emotion in the larger numbers known as

spectators. Emotion and excitement can be transferred from one individual to another.

In *II Corinthians 9*, Paul wrote about a group of believers and their concern in the giving of gifts to help the saints in need. Listen to Paul's testimony about their giving, *"For I know the forwardness of your mind, for which I boast of you to them of Macedonia, that Achaia was ready a year ago; and your zeal hath provoked very many" (II Corinthians 9:2)*. Over a year prior to this, when the need was made known, these believers had a readiness and willingness of mind to provide for those in need. Their eagerness so touched the heart of Paul that when he related the story in Macedonia, it invoked an abundant response in them. The zeal of giving at Achaia stimulated giving in those at Macedonia. This was no small stimulation, for Paul said it provoked *"very many."* Paul literally said "your zeal has stimulated many, many!"

What are our actions encouraging others to do? Every one of us has a positive or negative effect on those about us. Paul said in *Romans 14:7, "For none of us liveth to himself, and no man dieth to himself."*

Simon was a Zealot, one consumed with a passionate desire for his country. There was no cost too high and no sacrifice too great when it came to driving the enemy from their borders. God harnessed that zeal and turned Simon's focus toward the Savior and the things of God. The Zealot became a zealous Christian.

How sad that a people with "in God we trust" on their money is so far removed from Him. James Golder Burns wrote, concerning the British Isles, "Is it entirely to the credit of a country professing Christianity that it should worship the trinity of commerce, politics, and sports with such manifestations of devotion, while its Christian temples are deserted?" Our world is filled with zeal, only it is misdirected and ignorant.

While it breaks the heart to see this condition prevalent in the world, even worse is its prevalence in the life of believers. The same individual that will put the number of their favorite race car driver on their car would not dare be caught with a religious symbol on their car. The same person that would drive two hundred miles, fight a crowd of thousands, and spend three hundred dollars that weekend to see a sporting event would not tolerate being crowded at church, would not drive twenty miles to revival, nor give one hundred dollars to missions.

Where are our Spiritual Zealots of today? Where are the Moodys, the John Bunyans, the Spurgeons, and the Martin Luthers of our day?

A man walked down the street carrying a sign. It read, "I am a fool for Christ." People laughed and snickered until they read the back of the sign, "Who's fool are you?"

Chapter Twelve

Judas, the Faulty Christian

Matthew 26:14-16 "Then one of the twelve, called Judas Iscariot, went unto the chief priests, And said unto them, What will ye give me, and I will deliver him unto you? And they covenanted with him for thirty pieces of silver. And from that time he sought opportunity to betray him.

When one thinks of the name Judas, the mind immediately drifts toward the negative side of things. The name Judas stands last and lowest in the Apostolic list. In reading and studying this man's life I, endeavored to think of a word that would best describe how I perceived the man called Judas. The word that repetitively came to my mind was the word faulty. The word faulty has the idea of something impaired or defective, a weakness, offense, or mistake. Judas was a man proven to be impaired and defective in the Christian faith.

While it is not something that I take pleasure in saying, I feel that our churches are filled with "Faulty Christians." We all battle the old man in our Christian experience, but I am speaking of something far greater than that. I am speaking of a group of individuals that will go out into eternity with their name on a church roll but not in the Lamb's Book of Life. *"And I saw the dead, small and great, stand before God; and the books were opened: and another book was opened, which is the book of life: and the dead were judged out of those things which were written in the books, according to their works (Revelation 20:12).* I am speaking of individuals doped by Satan's devices, grasping for the pleasures of the world, thus causing them to be saved so as by fire. *"If any man's work shall be burned, he shall suffer loss:*

but he himself shall be saved; yet so as by fire" (I Corinthians 3:15).

As we carefully examine this man's life, may Judas serve as an example of what an individual does not want to be. May we contrast our lives with Judas, looking for areas that would prove to be faulty. If likeness appears, may the fear of similar results cause us to quickly run to Calvary and plunge beneath its cleansing flow!

The Covering of the Faulty Christian
Matthew 26:21-22
When it was announced that one would betray the Lord, everyone was surprised that it was Judas. *"When Jesus had thus said, he was troubled in spirit, and testified, and said, Verily, verily, I say unto you, that one of you shall betray me. Then the disciples looked one on another, doubting of whom he spake" (John 13:21-22).* Only two people knew the identity of the betrayer, Judas and Jesus. *"For Jesus knew from the beginning who they were that believed not, and who should betray him" (John 6:64).*

There is nothing that can be hidden from the omniscience of the Lord Jesus. We are known to Him **physically**, *"But the very hairs of your head are all numbered" (Matthew 10:30),* **mentally**, *"And Jesus knew their thoughts" (Matthew 12:25),* and **spiritually**, *"And needed not that any should testify of man: for he knew what was in man" (John 2:25).*

While Judas had covered himself with enough religious facade to be undetected by those about him, those things could not hide his betrayal from the Lord. What was true for Judas then is true for us today. Nothing can be hidden from God! It does not matter how elaborate or whitewashed our religious sepulchers; at best, they are filled with dead men's bones.

1. A Name

Judas went undetected to some because he had a good name. Listen to the words of Leslie Flynn from his book, The Twelve, "Judas started out well. His beginning had all the elements of nobility. Judas was once a proud name, a form of Judah, which means praised. Judas Maccabaeus, who led his people in revolt against their Macedonian oppressors, was a great national hero like George Washington. Jesus had a brother named Judas." Judas was a name that Jewish fathers and mothers were honored to place on their sons.

While Judas may have had a good name, it did not hide the fact that his heart was corrupt. Many today try to hide behind the name Christian! Just because one may possess the name Christian, it does not mean one possesses the nature of a Christian. Followers of Jesus Christ were *"called Christians first at Antioch" (Acts 11:26)*. This name was not to distinguish a nationality, but rather, a nature that had only been seen in the one they called Christ. It was given to His followers in a time of adversity and persecution. In a time that brings out the worst in most, it brought out the best in the believers at Antioch. Judas, as well as many others, tried to hide behind a name. When speaking to the church at Sardis, God said, *"I know thy works, that thou hast a name that thou livest, and art dead" (Revelation 3:1)*. They had a name but not the nature to go with it. We should not be asking "what's your name?" but "what's your nature?"

2. A Family

From what we can determine, Judas came from a good home and was a descendant of extraordinarily fine people. It is thought that he came from Kerioth, a small town a few miles south of Hebron. How many times have you heard it said of a young person that has gone astray, "I don't understand it. They come from such a good family, and none of their people were that way."

Being a member of a good family is no guarantee of salvation nor of being in a right relationship with God. Thank God for the blessing of being brought up in a Christian home where one has the privileges of being introduced to the Word of God, prayer, church, and the precious things of God. But, being a member of a Christian home does not mean that you are saved or walking in the will of God for your life. Salvation and living a separated life is a personal matter. Quite possibly, Judas tried to cover the corruption of his heart by the fact that he came from a good family.

3. A Position

Judas was perceived as more than just a believer. He was not only a member of the twelve, he had been chosen to be the treasurer for the group. He managed and dispersed their funds as needed. Surely there was no way he was the one to betray Christ. Didn't an elite position among the twelve mean anything? Is there any way a man could fill a pulpit and be lost? Could the lofty positions in the church be occupied by men and women that have never had a personal relationship with Christ? Could our religious leadership be consumed with lust of the flesh, lust of the eyes, and the pride of life *(see 1 John 2:16)*? The answer to all of the above is "Yes." When speaking of heaven and the judgment to come, Jesus said, *"Many will say to me in that day, Lord, Lord, have we not prophesied in thy name? and in thy name have cast out devils? and in thy name done many wonderful works? And then will I profess unto them, I never knew you: depart from me, ye that work iniquity" (Matthew 7:22-23).* It is not your position in the religious superstructure; rather, it is one's personal relationship with Christ that assures one of heaven.

One old preacher said, "Two things will surprise those that get to heaven. First, those that got to heaven that they thought wouldn't make it. Secondly, those that didn't make it that they thought would."

The last person the disciples thought possible of selling out the Son of God was Judas. He had covered his tracks well. But, not well enough! For there was one that knew his heart better than Judas knew his own heart, it was the Lord Jesus. The Lord's knowledge and understanding of hearts is not just limited to Judas, but He has full understanding of all men's physical, mental, and spiritual conditions. He knows all about you and me. What are you trying to cover from the eyes of others?

The Crime of a Faulty Christian
Matthew 26:14-16
Judas went to the chief priests and bargained with them to sell out the Son of God for thirty pieces of silver, the price of a common slave *(Exodus 21:32)*. There are two terms used to describe the crime of Judas, deliver and betray. In the Greek, they are the same word. The original word means to surrender, yield up, betray, bring forth, or give over. The crime of Judas was loving something more than he loved the Saviour. When Judas was made to choose between the two, he surrendered and yielded up the Lord Jesus Christ. What would you choose over the Son of God? Or, maybe the question should be what have you chosen over the Saviour?

1. Possessions
Judas was a covetous man. From several recorded events, we are permitted to see his lustful heart. In John's record of Mary anointing the Lord with the pound of spikenard, a very costly ointment, Judas responded by saying, *"Why was not this ointment sold for three hundred pence, and given to the poor" (John 12:5)?* This sounded very religious, and one would think it was the response of a heart tender toward the needs of others. God pulled the covers back and said, *"This he said, not that he cared for the poor; but because he was a thief, and had the bag, and bare what was put therein" (vs. 6).* The sale of the ointment would have netted a profit of three hundred pence and would have went into the treasury. Judas was more interested in money than in God being worshipped and lavished with costly treasure.

In John's description of Judas, two phrases are used to reveal another aspect of Judas' nature. Both are in *verse 6, "he was a thief"* and *"had the bag and bare what was put therein."* The first statement is fairly plain, while the second is a little more hidden. When John said that Judas *bare what was put therein,* the word "bare" means to carry, but it also has the idea of to pilfer. It is like the word lift, it can mean to carry or to steal. Judas was stealing a little from the general fund all the time.

The final straw was when Judas went to the chief priests and bargained with them for thirty pieces of silver. This was the price for which Judas would sell out. For what price are we willing to sell out? Leslie Flynn tells the story of a farmer who drove his truck onto the grain elevator scales, then stepped over on the scales himself. Seeing what the man had done, the operator went ahead and recorded the total weight on the scales credit form. Handing it to the farmer, he remarked, "you just sold yourself for $10.00." I have heard it said, "every man has his price." I hate to think that is true! I would rather believe that most would retain their integrity until death. I know one that did, and His name was Jesus. May we follow in His steps.

Judas was faced with choosing between possessions and the Saviour. Like the rich young ruler, Judas chose monetary wealth over spiritual wealth *(see Matthew 19 & Mark 10).* What choice have you made, money or the Master?

2. Praise
There is some evidence that Judas sold out for the praise and popularity of men. Could Judas have felt that he was not getting the praise and attention that he deserved? The first bit of light comes from Judas' name. Most say that the name Judas means praise. Now remember that this was a name given him by his parents. The name of an individual revealed something about them. Did the parents of Judas see something in him they thought worthy of praise? When that praise was not coming

148

from those about him, he sought it with the religious hierarchy. Solomon said of pride, *"Pride goeth before destruction, and an haughty spirit before a fall. Better it is to be of an humble spirit with the lowly, than to divide the spoil with the proud"* *(Proverbs 16:18-19)*. When listing the sins of Sodom, pride is one of the first mentioned *(see Ezekiel 16:49)*. We are told that God hates six things, yea seven, and the first on the list is a *"proud look" (Proverbs 6:17)*. Do we seek the praises of men above the approval of the Saviour?

While Judas occupied the position of treasurer, he never made the inner circle. He was never permitted to participate in any special events. Some have felt that even though Judas was one of the twelve, he still felt like an outsider. If Judas was from Kerioth, south of Hebron, it would have meant that he was the only non-Galilean *(Joshua 15:25)*. While chosen of the Lord and given the bag, Judas may have never felt like part of the group. One that just never did measure up to the other's standards. Thus, he turned away from Christ to seek the praise of others. Judas desired to be a somebody with men rather than a servant for Christ. Will we sell out truth and convictions to fit in rather than stand alone for Christ?

We have recorded for us this account in Luke's gospel, *"Then entered Satan into Judas surnamed Iscariot, being of the number of the twelve" (Luke 22:3)*. The word "entered" means to enter, arise, or come in. What greater door of opportunity for Satan to enter into one's life than the doorway of pride. It was pride that led to the fall of Satan himself. *"How art thou fallen from heaven, O Lucifer, son of the morning! how art thou cut down to the ground, which didst weaken the nations! For thou hast said in thine heart, I will ascend into heaven, I will exalt my throne above the stars of God: I will sit also upon the mount of the congregation, in the sides of the north: I will ascend above the heights of the clouds; I will be like the most High" (Isaiah 14:12-14)*. When an individual is consumed with the praise of men, the Devil has a large door of opportunity to enter or greatly influence one's life. The Bible tells us that the fear of man bringeth a snare *(Proverbs 29:25)*, but let us not forget that the applause of men can bring the same results.

3. Personal Desires
Some have suggested that Judas was part of the *Sikarios,* a violent and fanatical nationalist group that had pledged to use any means to drive the Romans from Palestine. William McIntyre said, "Judas was not from Galilee as the other disciples, but was a native of Judea where Jewish patriotism reached its height." Judas would then have had national goals for Israel and not spiritual goals. Judas would not have seen freedom and liberty in the death of the Saviour but rather in the rise of a Sovereign. Judas could not and would not die to his own personal desires.

Some have suggested that the turning point in Judas' life came when the people were going to take Jesus by force and make Him king *(John 6:15).* Jesus departed out of the midst of the people into a mountain alone to avoid it. Judas began to realize that Jesus was not going to fight for the throne of Israel. Just a few verses later Jesus said, *"Have not I chosen you twelve, and one of you is a devil" (John 6:70)?* The seed of rebellion had begun to flourish in the life of Judas.

If Jesus was not going to take the throne by force, Judas was going to force Him to by selling Him out to the chief priests. Then, Jesus would have to fight, and Judas would get what he wanted. Judas may have accepted a warring Sovereign but not a crucified Saviour! Judas' personal desires took precedent over even the will of God.

Listen to the words of J.D. Jones, "the problem was not that Judas was not sincere in following Christ, but that he was not whole-hearted in his devotion. Judas did not leave all to follow Christ." Judas was a man with a divided allegiance. James warns us about divided allegiance. *"A double minded man is unstable in all his ways" (James 1:8).* A two-spirited man is inconstant in all of his ways and will vacillate in his opinion and purpose. Judas was without a doubt a man of weakness. He yielded to possessions, praise, and personal desires. Judas could not hold on to what he wanted and hold onto Christ too. He was driven to choose between the two. So, Judas sold out the Son of God and his own soul in the same deal. *"No man can serve two masters: for either he will hate the one, and love the other; or else he will hold to the one, and despise the other. Ye cannot serve God and mammon" (Matthew 6:24).* J.D. Jones points out that Matthew the publican and Judas were on two parallel roads, both having a love for money. Yet, they ended worlds apart because Matthew left all to follow Jesus and Judas followed with a divided heart. To whom have you given your heart?

The Cure for a Faulty Christian
John 6:70-71
Judas is not the only Apostle that Jesus called a devil. When Jesus began to reveal the cross and the death He must suffer, Peter took Jesus and began to rebuke Him *(Matthew 16:22).* Listen to the response of our Lord, *"But he turned, and said unto Peter, Get thee behind me, Satan: thou art an offence unto me: for thou savourest not the things that be of God, but those that be of men. Then said Jesus unto his disciples, If any man will come after me, let him deny himself, and take up his cross, and follow me. For whosoever will save his life shall lose it: and whosoever will lose his life for my sake shall find it" (Matthew 16:23-25).* If both Simon Peter and Judas were called devils, why was their end so radically different? The answer to that question is a simple one. While both men were reprimanded by the Saviour, Peter responded with repentance while Judas responded with resentment.

On numerous occasions, Jesus tried to warn Judas of his impending doom. Judas proved to be a man void of wisdom. *"A wise man will hear, and will increase learning; and a man of understanding shall attain unto wise counsels" (Proverbs 1:5)*

"Reprove not a scorner, lest he hate thee: rebuke a wise man, and he will love thee. Give instruction to a wise man, and he will be yet wiser: teach a just man, and he will increase in learning" *(Proverbs 9:8-9).* Judas would not respond to the warning of Christ. May we pause and ask ourselves if we too are void of wisdom when it comes to responding to the admonishments of the Saviour. Have our hearts become hardened to His word and His will?

There are at least four times in John's writings that Jesus tried to get Judas' attention. After the feeding of the five thousand, the people were going to take Jesus by force and make Him king. Jesus slipped away into the mountain alone. When Jesus began to reveal the necessity of His death to His followers, many of them turned and walked with Him no more *(John 6:66).* It was then that Jesus gave the warning of falling away. *"Jesus answered them, Have not I chosen you twelve, and one of you is a devil" (John 6:70)?* Jesus was very explicit, *"one of you is a devil."* Why didn't Judas, as well as the other disciples, ask who it was? Why not respond to the warnings of God before the heart is callused and it is too late?

Jesus gathered with His disciples for the feast of Passover. After supper, Jesus laid aside His garments, took the place of a servant, and began to wash the feet of the disciples. In an explanation of what this act meant, Jesus said, *"He that is washed needeth not save to wash his feet, but is clean every whit: and ye are clean, but not all" (John 13:10).* I wonder if Jesus looked straight at Judas when He said, *"but not all?"* Still, no one asked who the unclean disciple was. Judas' heart was still unmoved.

None of the disciples seemed to be moved by the Lord's warnings, so Jesus began a discourse on the Scriptures. The Word of God speaks of one from our midst that will betray the Son of God. Then, in a straightforward manner, Jesus said,

"Verily, verily, I say unto you, that one of you shall betray me" *(John 13:21).* Judas turned to the Lord and said, *"Master is it I"* *(Matthew 26:25)?* Jesus then said to Judas, *"Thou hast said."* Jesus had confronted Judas face to face and still no repentance.

The final effort to turn Judas from the way of ruin was a gester of kindness. At the Passover meal, among other things, there were three things on the table. There was a paste made of apples, dates, pomegranates, and nuts. This was called the charosheth. Secondly, there were bitter herbs such as endive, horseradish, chicory, and horehound. The paste was a reminder of the bricks they made under slavery, and the herbs reminded them of the bitterness of slavery. There was also unleavened bread which the host would take two pieces of and put some bitter herbs between. He would then dip it in the charosheth. This was called the sop. It was a very great honor for the host to make up a sop and personally give it to a guest. It spoke of one being an honored guest. Jesus gave the sop to Judas, and he was unmoved by the gester of kindness.

Listen carefully to the words of Gaston Foote, "the road signs, after two thousand years, are the same for all pilgrims along the way. Repentance means life; resentment means death. Judas was the only disciple whom Jesus could not transform. He stumbled into outer darkness, from resentment to ruin." Will this be the story of your life? Do the warnings of God and the kindness of God create resentment or remorse?

Judas proved to be impaired and defective in the Christian faith. He could not embrace Christ because he was unwilling to let go of the things of the world. When it came to a choice between the two, Judas sold out the Son of God. Do you have a price? If you do, the Devil will meet it. Listen to these words of Jesus, *"For what is a man profited, if he shall gain the whole world, and lose his own soul? or what shall a man give in exchange for his soul"*

(Matthew 16:26)? Have you sold out to Satan or to the Saviour? One means eternal ruin, while the other means eternal rewards. Are you a **Faulty Christian**?

Chapter Thirteen

Paul, the Suffering Christian

Romans 1:1 "Paul, a servant of Jesus Christ, called to be an apostle, separated unto the gospel of God."
Acts 9:11&15-16 "And the Lord said unto him, Arise, and go into the street which is called Straight, and inquire in the house of Judas for one called Saul, of Tarsus: for, behold, he prayeth . . . But the Lord said unto him, Go thy way: for he is a chosen vessel unto me, to bear my name before the Gentiles, and kings, and the children of Israel: "For I will show him how great things he must suffer for my name's sake."

One of the most dynamic and dedicated Christians of recorded history was the Apostle Paul. Some have tried to say that Paul was not an apostle. In order to discredit the message of grace, the Judizers tried to say that Paul was not called or qualified to be an apostle. While giving evidence of the resurrection, Paul told of his call to be an apostle in *I Corinthians 15:8-10. "And last of all he was seen of me also, as of one born out of due time. For I am the least of the apostles, that am not meet to be called an apostle, because I persecuted the church of God. But by the grace of God I am what I am: and his grace which was bestowed upon me was not in vain; but I laboured more."* In nine of the books which God used Paul to write, he opened the letter using the little phrase *"Paul . . . an apostle" (Romans 1:1).*

While studying the life of this great man, it becomes evident that there are many subjects which could be discussed. All of them would prove to be worthy of study and would definitely be beneficial to any student of the Word. But, one of the overshadowing truths that surfaces continually in Paul's life is suffering. While defending his call of God, he listed some of the things that he endured for the cause of Christ. *"Are they ministers of Christ? (I speak as a fool) I am more; in labours more abundant, in stripes above measure, in prisons more frequent, in deaths oft. Of the Jews five times received I forty stripes save one. Thrice was I beaten with rods, once was I stoned, thrice I suffered shipwreck, a night and a day I have been in the deep; In journeyings often, in perils of waters, in perils of robbers, in perils by mine own countrymen, in perils by the heathen, in perils in the city, in perils in the wilderness, in perils in the sea, in perils among false brethren; In weariness and painfulness, in watchings often, in hunger and thirst, in fastings often, in cold and nakedness. Beside those things that are without, that which cometh upon me daily, the care of all the churches"* (I Corinthians 11:23-28).

While we do not like to accept it, suffering is part of the Christian life. One of the age-old questions is, Why do good people suffer? We do not understand everything going wrong when we are trying to do everything right. To the numerous questions about suffering, I do not believe there are any simple answers. Each of us must trust God during those times of difficulty and appropriate the grace that is available from the hand of our loving Heavenly Father.

Even though we do not have all the answers when it comes to suffering, we are given many truths through the life of the Apostle Paul which can aid us in these difficult times. Paul did not resist the suffering but marched forward by God's grace. Paul's suffering can encourage each of us and give us divine light that will help generate peace in our times of adversity. Look with me at Paul, the suffering Christian.

The Providence of Suffering
Acts 9:16 "he must suffer"
One of the greatest insights into suffering is through an understanding of providence in relationship to suffering. In the

record of the Apostle Paul's conversion, great light is shed on this subject. For the most effect and understanding, it is needful to read *Acts 9:1-23.*

For three days Paul sat in the blackness of blindness void of food or understanding. God was working openly and behind the scenes in the life of Paul. How it is needful to grasp this truth! God works in each of our lives both seen and unseen. Unaware that God was doing anything, Paul mused his condition while the whole time God was preparing a servant to minister to his needs. God was directing Ananias on the way to Paul and with the words for Paul. This fact should help us to understand that suffering is not for our grief but for our good and His Glory!

In preparing Ananias for this mission, God calms, commissions, and communicates with him *(see Acts 9:13-16).* Please note what God tells Ananias about the man he was being sent to minister. *"For I will show him how great things he must suffer for my name's sake" (Acts 9:16).* Blindness is only the beginning of Paul's suffering! God's forecast for the future was not just suffering but great suffering. It does not take a great theologian to grasp what the future holds for this dear child of God. But, one must realize that Paul's future is also ours. *"But the God of all grace, who hath called us unto his eternal glory by Christ Jesus, after that ye have suffered a while, make you perfect, stablish, strengthen, settle you" (I Peter 5:10). "Confirming the souls of the disciples, and exhorting them to continue in the faith, and that we must through much tribulation enter into the kingdom of God" (Acts 14:22).* Being a Christian does not exempt you from suffering, heartache, and tribulation of the world. It is in the providence of God that we are called to suffer.

It was God that chose the path that Paul would travel, and that path would be filled with suffering. Paul, like most of us, would not have chosen this painful way. While it was a painful way, it was also a perfecting way! There are two truths that are manifested in the providence of suffering. God chooses:

1. The Diversity of Suffering

Suffering comes in many shapes, sizes, and shades. In *II Corinthians 11:24-28,* the diversity of suffering is seen in the life of Paul. In *verses 24-26,* Paul listed for us the physical suffering that he was confronted with as a believer and servant of Christ. The physical suffering consisted of being whipped, beaten with a rod, stoned and left for dead, shipwrecked, and a multitude of perils. Paul suffered extreme physical abuse for the cause of Christ. Paul also received a physical thorn in the flesh from the hand of the Lord Himself. There is a lot of conjecture as to what it was, but this we do know, it was a physical limitation. *Hebrews 11* records for us saints that suffered for the cause of Christ. *"And others had trial of cruel mockings and scourgings, yea, moreover of bonds and imprisonment: They were stoned, they were sawn asunder, were tempted, were slain with the sword: they wandered about in sheepskins and goatskins; being destitute, afflicted, tormented; (Of whom the world was not worthy:) they wandered in deserts, and in mountains, and in dens and caves of the earth" (Hebrews 11:36-38).* We too are faced with physical suffering! Fanny J. Crosby suffered blindness from early childhood because a doctor placed the wrong medication in her eyes. Your body may be disfigured because of some accident, or it may be deteriorating because of some terrible disease. While we may not know the why, we can rest assured that it is in the providence of a loving Heavenly Father.

In *verse 27,* when Paul spoke of *"weariness and painfulness, in watchings,"* the emphasis was toward the mental aspect of suffering. This suffering has its effects on the mind which also affects the body. The idea of this phrase is toil that reduces strength and produces sadness because one has tried to remain awake or watch. These vigils are the result of threats on Paul's life by the enemies of God. This produces a mental and physical anguish that cannot be separated. Sometimes the mental anguish is worse than the personal physical suffering. In the world today, there is the mental stress in the work place as well as the pressures associated with family life. Parents are mentally drained as they contemplate the future of their children. Then, there is the mental pressure associated with finances.

Paul also made reference to spiritual suffering in *verse 28* when he said, *"Beside those things that are without, that which cometh upon me daily, the care of all the churches."* Paul had a love for both the saved and the lost. Listen to these words, *"For I could wish that myself were accursed from Christ for my brethren, my kinsmen according to the flesh" (Romans 9:3).* Paul loved his people and desired that they come to the saving knowledge of the Lord Jesus Christ. He prayed that they would cease from being the enemy of Christ and embrace Him as Lord and Saviour. If he cared this much for those outside the church, just imagine how he felt about those infant churches that he had been given the privilege to start. This love and interest can be seen when he approached Barnabas about visiting the churches, *"Let us go again and visit our brethren in every city where we have preached the word of the Lord, and see how they do" (Acts 15:36).* If one will take time to read the letters Paul wrote to the churches, it becomes obvious at the number of times his heart is broken over their failures and waywardness. Only another preacher of the gospel can relate to the spiritual suffering of the ministry. There is the spiritual suffering of wayward children, lost loved ones, and personal spiritual warfare.

2. The Duration of Suffering

Not only does God determine the diversity, but He is also in charge of the duration. Some of Paul's suffering was momentary. The shipwreck lasted a night and a day. There were times that the physical suffering may have lasted weeks or even months. I would not think a week would be enough time to get over being stoned and left for dead. There is some suffering in Paul's life that came and went with time, but the thorn in the flesh was for a lifetime. None of us know to what extent we will suffer. All is in the providence of the Master.

How did Paul respond to the different elements and situations in which he found himself in pain? *"Not that I speak in respect of want: for I have learned, in whatsoever state I am, therewith to be content" (Philippians 4:11).* May each of us bow our heads and yield in submission unto the will of God for our lives as not only Paul did but our Saviour, the Lord Jesus Christ. *"Nevertheless not my will, but thine, be done" (Luke 22:42).*

The Purpose of Suffering
Acts 9:16 "my name's sake"
When one is caused to think that there could be a purpose for suffering, we are prone to immediately reject the idea. To think that any good could come out of suffering, that's out of the question! Each of us are programmed to view suffering as the result of something bad. Let us remember, while the process may not be palatable, the purpose can be good and honorable. An example of this is using physical correction when a child has done wrong. *"Foolishness is bound in the heart of a child; but the rod of correction shall drive it far from him" (Proverbs 22:15).* The purpose is not to harm the child but to help the child. Suffering can have a rewarding purpose. Was this the case with Paul and the numerous things he suffered? Yes! There are three areas I want to look at where God had a positive purpose by permitting suffering.

1. Salvation to the Sinner
Take a close look at Saul before his salvation experience. In his hand was a fist full of warrants, in his heart was a fire of destruction, and in his head was the idea that he was doing God a great service by crushing all those found in the way *(see Acts 9:2).* What method did God use to awaken the heart of this religiously lost man? It could not have been schooling for he was educated beyond reason. God used suffering! Driven to the earth by a bright light that left him totally blind, Saul cried out, *"Who art thou, Lord" (Acts 9:5).* Through the means of suffering, God had gotten Saul's undivided attention. Suffering had taken a man

driven by hate and turned him into one being led by the hand. God knew what it would take to shake Saul lose from his sin, it was suffering.

While I do not cherish the thoughts, I know of cases where suffering was the instrument that God used to awaken the heart of lost individuals. Suffering deals in reality. The lost realize how fragile life is and turn their hearts toward eternity. When one realizes the eternal value of the soul, any degree or duration of suffering would be worth it if the individual came to know Christ as personal Saviour. The strength of this truth can be seen in *Matthew 5:29-30. "For it is profitable for thee that one of thy members should perish, and not that thy whole body should be cast into hell."*

2. Salutations to the Saviour
The Lord was going to show Paul the many things he would suffer. What was to be the purpose of this suffering? *"Bear my name before . . . my name sake" (Acts 9:15-16).* This suffering servant was going to bear the name of Christ throughout the known world. The word bear means to lift, declare, carry, and to take up. There is a promise associated with lifting up the Lord Jesus Christ. *"And I, if I be lifted up from the earth, will draw all men unto me" John 12:32).* The suffering of Paul would give him privileges and opportunities to lift up the name of Christ in places others could never have witnessed! Shipwreck got the attention of those sailing with Paul to Rome *(see Acts 27).* Snakebite allowed Paul to witness to a heathen tribe *(see Acts 28).* The chains of Rome let Paul declare the greatness of the Saviour throughout the entire empire. When we are faced with suffering, may we seek an avenue to exalt and lift up the name of our Saviour. In many cases, our greatest ally in advancing the kingdom may be our own personal suffering.

3. Sanctification of the Saint
If the child of God is not very careful, they can become filled with pride. Sometimes we allow our blessings and talents to

become a deterrent to our service for Him. Rather than bearing His name, we begin to exalt self and its virtues. Paul warned of this problem in *Romans 12:3, "For I say, through the grace given unto me, to every man that is among you, not to think of himself more highly than he ought to think; but to think soberly, according as God hath dealt to every man the measure of faith."* The word highly means to esteem oneself over much, to be vain or arrogant. What will take the wind out of pride quicker than anything else? Suffering! Suffering brings us back in touch with our humanity.

Paul told us that this was the reason God gave him a thorn in the flesh. *"And lest I should be exalted above measure through the abundance of the revelations, there was given to me a thorn in the flesh, the messenger of Satan to buffet me, lest I should be exalted above measure" (II Corinthians 12:7).* Paul knew that the Lord had given him many privileges, and those privileges could cause him to become haughty or cause him to raise himself to a lofty position. The suffering of the thorn was preventative medicine. What Paul knew, we must some time accept by faith. Our Heavenly Father not only loves us but knows what is best for us.

While we do not like the taste of suffering, the purpose is a good one when it is approved and appointed by God. Planted in the soil of omnipotence and growing from the stem of providence, suffering has a lofty and holy purpose.

The Product of Suffering
II Corinthians 12:9
Not only is there a purpose to suffering but that purpose yields a product. Remember the example of physical correction in *Proverbs 22:15?* The physical suffering yields good results. The product in this case is a child whose heart or life is not filled with folly. Suffering in the life of the Apostle Paul yielded several products, two of which I want to magnify.

1. Humility

Since the fall of Adam in the garden, one of the outstanding marks of man's depravity is pride. To some extent, it was pride that caused man to respond to the lies of Satan. In this state of depravity, the heart of man desires to exalt itself, to rise up even above his Creator. Pride is not only sin, but it is something God hates. *"These six things doth the LORD hate: yea, seven are an abomination unto him: A proud look, a lying tongue, and hands that shed innocent blood" (Proverbs 6:16-17).* Pride holds God at a distance and makes fellowship impossible. One thing that will dispel pride from the heart of man the quickest is suffering! Suffering vanquishes the banners of war and elevates the white flags of surrender.

God desired to produce **humility in the life of a sinner.** If one will carefully read the first part of *Acts 9,* it will become apparent that there was a man that was assertive. Saul knew what he wanted, and would do anything to attain his objective. Saul had his heart as well as his fist raised against the Lord Jesus Christ and His church. In this state, God had not been able to get Saul's attention. After Saul had been smitten by the light and had fallen to the ground, he was led like a child *(see verses 8&11).* The fist is no longer clinched and the body erect, but Saul reached into the darkness for guidance and stooped in prayer for mercy. While the exact details may be different, many individuals have been humbled by the tool of suffering. When nothing else seemed to work, the hammer of suffering had broken the stonyhearted sinner. While the blow of the hammer may at first appear cruel, one must remember that the hands of love hold it, and the Eternal God of Glory has ordered the event. The product will be worth the punishment!

God desired to produce **humility in the life of a saint.** Paul knew that he had been abundantly blessed. In *II Corinthians 12: 7,* he spoke of the *"abundance of revelations."* Paul had been permitted by God to see, hear, and experience things that would generate envy in the lives of others. In *verses 2-4,* Paul spoke of an event in which he heard words that could not be uttered. All of these blessings and privileges have a way of making one proud and pharisaical. What tool will crush that pride and drive it from one's heart? Suffering! Paul tells us that God allowed him to suffer with the thorn in the flesh for the express purpose of dispelling pride. *"And lest I should be exalted above measure through the abundance of the revelations, there was given to me a thorn in the flesh, the messenger of Satan to buffet me, lest I should be exalted above measure" (II Corinthians 12:7).*

Paul was aware of the fact that God wanted to produce humility in his heart. Unlike Paul, most of us are not so discerning. Most of us would be eaten up with pride if it were not for the mercy and wisdom of God. *"O the depth of the riches both of the wisdom and knowledge of God! how unsearchable are his judgments, and his ways past finding out" (Romans 11:33)!* Because God knows us better than we know ourselves, He adjusts the thermostat of suffering to match the condition of our heart. What a great God we serve!

2. Strength
While it is beyond what the human mind can comprehend, suffering produces strength. We perceive suffering as a detriment to our health and strength, but while certain areas are weakening, others are gaining strength and momentum. It is imperative to remember that we are not speaking of a physical product that is produced by the individual but a divine strength and enablement. In examining Paul's suffering, there are two areas in which strength was produced.

In *II Corinthians 12:9,* Paul found that the thorn in the flesh had produced **strength for the way.** After repetitively asking for the removal of this thorn of suffering, the Lord told Paul two things, *"My grace is sufficient for thee"* and *"my strength is made perfect in weakness."* The grace of God allowed Paul to trade human strength for divine strength, but the means by which this divine strength came was suffering. Paul realized the tremendous opportunity and blessing before him, and he responded with total approval to God's will. *"Most gladly therefore will I rather glory in my infirmities, that the power of Christ may rest upon me."* What Paul could not face or endure in his own strength, he could pass through with the Lord's strength.

Paul came to realize that suffering was not to deter him in the way but aid him in the Christian journey. What was true for Paul is true for each of us! The strength that we need comes by abiding in Him. Abiding in Him means that there will be times of suffering. In *John 15:2,* Jesus tells about the purging of the vine. To the human mind, the process may appear painful and unneeded. Why subject the vine to suffering the purging process while it is producing fruit? The purpose is not to weaken the vine but provide strength to produce more fruit. It is through the pain of removal that more fruit comes forth from the vine. It is this abundant fruit bearing that brings glory to our heavenly Father. *"Herein is my Father glorified, that ye bear much fruit" (John 15:8).* The suffering which God permits to come our way is not to harm us but to help us.

Suffering in the life of Paul would produce **strength for a witness.** After Paul had been smitten with blindness on the Damascus road, he was led by the hand into the city. For three days he was without food, drink, or sight *(see Acts 9:9).* It was during this suffering that Saul was getting weaker, and Paul was getting stronger. Paul had a visit from Ananias, God's prepared servant. Paul received his sight, was filled with the Holy Ghost, and was baptized as a testimony to his acceptance of Christ as Saviour. What did this suffering produce in Saul's life besides salvation? *"And straightway he preached Christ in the synagogues, that he is the Son of God" (Acts 9:20).* Suffering produced a witness for the Lord Jesus Christ. But, this was not just some weak, passive witness. Listen to *verses 22-23, "But Saul increased the more in strength, and confounded the Jews which dwelt at Damascus, proving that this is very Christ. And after that many days were fulfilled, the Jews took counsel to kill* *him."* Paul had such a powerful witness for the Lord Jesus Christ that the Jews sought to kill him. Suffering had produced a witness that the religious educators could not resist or silence.

In many instances, it is our suffering that gives strength to our witness. When Paul listed for us all the things he suffered for the cause of Christ, it becomes evident to all that only God could bring an individual through all those things. It becomes a witness to the sufficiency of God's grace and His power. It is one thing to stand on this side of the furnace and tell how God can deliver; it is quite another to tell of His grace after passing through the fire. The three Hebrew lads' witness was strengthened by the fire. Your witness may gain strength only after a hospital stay, a trip to the graveyard, or some terrible financial reverse. May each of us see the advantages in suffering and yield to God's will for our lives.

The Power in Suffering
II Corinthians 12:9
When Paul first received the thorn in the flesh, he just knew God would delight in removing it. Paul assumed that the suffering that was associated with it meant that the thorn was of little or no value. Paul sought God often and intently for the removal of this nuisance for he knew he would be better off without the thorn. To Paul's surprise, the thorn would accompany him to the grave, and the thorn would prove to be a treasure. Rather than weakness, there was power in suffering. *"For my strength is made perfect in weakness" (verse 9).* The power of the thorn was not in transforming the suffering but in transforming the sufferer. The word perfect means to complete, or to consummate in character. The miraculous power of God would change the saint in the midst of the suffering. The power in suffering transformed three areas of Paul's life. These are seen in *verses 9 & 10* and are manifested in the three words; gladly, glory, and pleasure.

1. His Motives

When Paul first received the thorn, he was saddened by the suffering and his sole motivation was to rid himself of this discomfort. After a period of time, the power of the thorn began to transform Paul. Paul was motivated to embrace the thorn rather than to extract the thorn. This was revealed in the phrase, *"Most gladly therefore will I" (verse 9).* The word gladly means with great pleasure. The thorn of pain had now become a pleasure, and Paul was no longer motivated or preoccupied with getting rid of it. Paul was no longer motivated by the suffering but by the Saviour. Paul's eyes and his thoughts were upon the Lord that desired to bless him rather than to buffet him.

2. His Mouth

Paul's mouth had been filled with prayers pleading for the removal of this taxing burden! We are told that on three specific occasions, Paul implored and beseeched the Lord to remove the thorn. While most of his words may have been addressed to the Lord, some of his complaints may have been vocalized to the brethren. Paul may have bemoaned and rehearsed his plight before others. Could it be that the only thing Paul was talking about was how bad he was having it? Most of our prayer meeting services need to be renamed and called moaning services. Something had changed for Paul's lips no longer spoke of pain but of pleasure. Paul said, *"I rather glory in my infirmities" (verse 9).* Glory means to boast or rejoice. Paul was now praising the Saviour rather than pining about the suffering. If one is boasting, it requires others to hear it. Paul was rejoicing to the Saviour and rehearsing before the saints what great things God was doing.

3. His Mind

When the thorn came, Paul felt like God was against him, and Paul wanted to reject the suffering. Paul knew it was God's will, but he did not like it. Paul felt like things would be better if God changed His will to match Paul's will. I am ashamed to have to say it, but I react in the same manner. I want God to conform to my will. The thorn had sufficient power to transform the mind of Paul. He said, *"Therefore I take pleasure in infirmities, in reproaches, in necessities, in persecutions, in distresses for Christ's sake" (verse 10)*. The word pleasure means to think well of or to be willing. Paul had his mind transformed to conform to God's will rather than to push for his will. Paul not only approved of God's will for his life, but was pleased with it no matter what it may have involved.

Rationalization nor education could have transformed the motives, mouth, and mind of the Apostle Paul! Paul had been transformed by the divine power of God that was consummated in his character through the means of suffering. While suffering does involve pain, it also yields peace to those that will embrace the thorn rather than being preoccupied with its extraction.

Paul's future was one of suffering. Your future and my future will also contain a diversity of suffering. May each of us yield to the perfecting work of God. It will do us good and bring Him glory.